Explanatory of
Petroleum Market Volatility

By

Roshdy Ebrahim, Ph.D

Copyright © 2018 Roshdy Ebrahim

All right reserved

ISBN: 9781980789642

Preface

Oil and gas resources have provided much of the world's energy in the twentieth century and are expected to be an important part of the energy mix well into the twenty-first century. Currently, oil and gas provide approximately 63 % of primary energy consumption in Europe. However, energy security in the region remains a concern.

The concern is reinforced due to Europe's dependence on oil and gas from other regions. In addition, many commentators fear domestic oil and gas resource depletion will produce significant supply scarcities in the short term, i.e., well before 2020. Thus, the purpose of this analysis is to address the subject by estimating conventional and unconventional oil and gas supply cost curves for the region.

From an economic point of view, relative prices will determine the dominance of oil and natural gas versus other fuels. To give an example, a significant tax on carbon would increase the relative price of coal versus gas. This would lead to investment and technological advancement across the gas industry and thus induce substitution from coal to gas by decreasing the relative price of gas.

Oil is a lifeblood of the modern economy, and it makes up the largest part of the world's traded energy, some one-third of the total. In particular oil fuels nearly all the extensive, cheap transport that is a major contributor to today's efficient global economic activity, whether in the production of food or goods, or provision of the services that we rely on. As most people appreciate, if oil is not available in the short-term food does not get to the shops, nor workers to their jobs, and society is at risk. This was amply demonstrated during the European 'fuel protests' of 2000.

Contents

Preface 3

Contents 5

introduction 7

1. Oil Price Fluctuations 11

   1.1. Recent Changes in the World Economy and the Global Financial Crisis 18

   1.2. The Financial Crisis and Its Impact on the Carbon Price Dynamics 26

   1.3. THE FINANCIAL CRISIS AND THE OIL MARKET 28

   1.4. The Costs of the First Oil Shock 38

   1.5. Monetary Policy 60

   1.6. Secular Stagnation 68

   1.7. France as a Case Study 72

2. Worldwide Subsidies to Fossil Energy 79

   2.1. Subsidized prices or fiscal revenues? ... 94

   2.2. Gross royalty 97

   2.3. Monopoly and Competition in the Oil Industry 99

3. Natural Gas as a Game-Changer 102

4. environmental pollution 108

   4.1. Carbon Fuels and Climate: Facts and Uncertainties 117

4.2. Effect of Threat of Global Warming 128

4.3. Measuring the Impact of Regulatory Announcements on CO2 Returns............134

4.4. Does CO2 Emissions Performance Matter for Stock Prices?........................138

4.5. Information Assimilation in the European Carbon Market........................143

5. Carbon Taxation 149

   5.1. TAX SPINNING 151

   5.2. Corporate income tax....................152

   5.3. Special petroleum tax....................154

   5.4. Additional payments and measures 155

   5.5. Natural gas taxation 158

   5.6. Comparison of natural gas and oil taxation.......................................167

6. Depreciation and Depletion in Oil Production 173

   6.1. Decommissioning 176

7. Renewable Energy Targets and Carbon Pricing May Conflict 180

   7.1. Alternative Energy Sources...........181

8. The Geopolitics of Oil 187

8.1. The Financial Impact of Terrorist Attacks on the Value of the Oil and Gas Industry 196

8.2. The Militarization of Energy (In)Security 199

References 207

Biography of the author 210

introduction

Oil is widely used in different sectors including transportation, production, energy supply, and as a raw material in the production of petrochemical products; this is why it has great value and affects other energy sources.

Recent years have seen increasing attention being paid to the broad issues of energy security and climate change, which are of the utmost importance for the European Union and its member states. Energy security has become a heavily discussed topic due to rising energy demand worldwide, increasing import dependence in many European countries, geopolitical tensions and conflicts, the globalization of formerly regional markets, and the need for a regulatory and policy response. [1]

A possible forthcoming fossil fuel depletion, geopolitical instability, and competing energy demands from high-growth countries are only a short list of the emerging and long-standing energy issues for the EU. These challenges are strictly intertwined with the climate change issue. The objective of building a low-carbon economy in Europe implies a reduction in fossil fuel use in residential and

---

[1] Rossella Bardazzi • Maria Grazia Pazienza Alberto Tonini: European Energy and Climate Security. Springer International Publishing Switzerland 2016. P 1

industrial activities. This goal is consistent with the energy security strategy, which includes a moderation of energy demand, an improvement in energy efficiency, increases in domestic energy production through renewables, and the development of new technologies. Indeed, these are some of the pillars of the European Energy Security Strategy, which was approved by the European Commission in May 2014. This communication states very clearly that the strategy is 'an integral part of the 2030 policy framework on climate and energy. [1]

The First Oil Shock of 1973 arose out of this situation, when certain Arab countries decided to embargo the export of oil to the United States to counter its support for Israel.

While no more than a political gesture, lasting only a few months, it did demonstrate the key role of oil in the world economy. Prices rose fivefold, prompting a serious economic recession lasting for years.

But generally speaking, the world came to terms with the Arab–Israeli conflict as it simmered over the last decades of the twentieth

---

[1]Rossella Bardazzi • Maria Grazia Pazienza Alberto Tonini: European Energy and Climate Security. Springer International Publishing Switzerland 2016. P 2

century, before the tensions were reignited as described below. (1)

In the period leading up to the 2008 financial crisis, the vast majority of investors were too optimistic about the future. Property prices would keep rising; the world economy, turbo-charged by globalization, would keep growing; only blue skies lay ahead. Increasing share prices, and the growth in lending reflected these positive expectations. Eventually the reality of mounting mortgage defaults chipped away at the positive mood and was reinforced by the failures of some over-exposed funds and institutions like Bear Sterns. In late 2008, the failure of Lehman Brothers delivered the final nail in the coffin to any remaining optimism and darkness overwhelmed the financial system. Share prices crashed, lending fell, and financial companies previously thought to be safe got into trouble. Suddenly, no one knew what or whom to trust. Without the lifeblood of confidence, the financial system ground to a halt. Only unprecedented intervention by many governments— and the infusion of trillions of dollars, euro, yen, pounds, and other currencies conjured up by central banks—saved the day and pulled the world back from the brink of a new Great Depression. (2)

(^{1})C.J. Campbell: Campbell's Atlas of Oil and Gas Depletion. Colin J. Campbell and Alexander Wöstmann 2013. P 382

1. Oil Price Fluctuations

The past decades have demonstrated how volatile oil prices are and how responsive the trading market is to those prices. In January 1999, after Iraq was allowed to sell oil under the UN's Oil-for-Food program, its 300% increased production coincided with the Asian financial crisis, which reduced demand, resulting in the price of oil dropping to just above $10 per barrel. Oil prices began increasing in 2000, reaching over $20 per barrel by September then falling back again, before they started their upward climb in 2003. Th at ascent saw crude rise to over $40 per barrel by September 2004 and reach $70 per barrel in September 2005. By the end of 2007, the price was in the $90s and analysts were predicting it would pass the psychological benchmark of $100. In January 2008, it did so, and even topped $140 in July that year. Despite its meteoric rise, oil began slipping in the second half of 2008 and by December it had dropped below $40. Over 2009 and 2010, the price settled between $65 and $85 per barrel. Some analysts predicted that was an appropriate range to keep production at levels preventing a shortfall, but not high enough to exacerbate the global recession that had begun in 2008. Th e Arab Revolutions that began in December 2010, along with threats of sanctioning Iranian oil, drove up oil prices that

---

[2]Roger Boyd: Energy and the Financial System Springer Cham Heidelberg New York Dordrecht London 2013. P 53

year so that the average price in 2011 was $111—an all-time high annual average.

While consumers react negatively to high oil prices, there are benefits for producers that accompany high prices. After 2011 Venezuela's extra heavy oil (which had previously been too expensive to be considered commercially viable) came under contracts increasing Venezuela's proven reserves from 100 billion barrels in 2007 to almost 300 billion in 2012. At the same time, oil that would have been too expensive to produce at $50 per barrels was coming on line in the Gulf of Mexico, Canada and the North Sea. Th e high price also spurred exploration and Brazil, which had 11.2 billion barrels of proven reserves in 2006, saw them rise to 13 billion in 2014, making Brazil the world's ninth largest producer of petroleum and other liquids that year. West Africa experienced similar rises in reserves owing to exploration in the Gulf of Guinea. On top of it all, fracking technology became commercially viable bringing American oil and natural gas online. Ultimately, that meant more oil and gas was becoming available which brought about the 2014 price collapse.

Explanatory of Petroleum Market Volatility

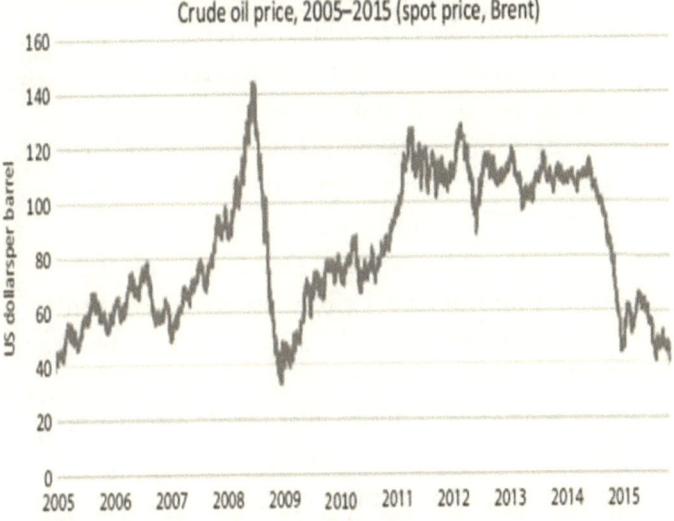

Oil prices are affected by a number of factors from the strength or weakness of the US dollar, to political instability, natural disasters, and speculation on the part of traders. Historically, prices have been very volatile, with gluts causing the price to plummet and shortages leading to steep rises. In the nineteenth century, the Standard Oil monopoly would sometimes flood the market with oil to force competing companies out of business and then readjust the price once the market was cleared of its competition. In the 1980s, as new independent producers appeared on the scene the price of a barrel nosedived by 70% in just a few months, from $31.75 per barrel of WTI in November 1985 to just $10 per barrel in 1986. That led

Saudi Arabia to adopt Standard Oil type tactics and let the price keep falling by relying on net-backing deals. Such deals guaranteed a fee to refiners per barrel and allowed the Saudis and refiners to split the profits, so they could get something per barrel even if the price was rock bottom. Th e Saudis knew—just as John D. Rockefeller of Standard Oil had—that they could afford to take a cut in profits if it forced some producers out of the market. In November 2014, the Saudis again refused to cut back on their production at the regular OPEC meeting in Vienna, preferring to retain their market share and figuring that eventually oil that was more expensive to produce would be forced out of the market while they preserved their market share.

Th e 2005–2008 spike in the price of crude had less to do with any one event than a convergence of factors. Th e war in Iraq was often touted as a reason, but the fact was that Iraq's production had been offline for much of the 1990s owing to the UN embargo imposed on Baghdad after its invasion of Kuwait in 1990. Th us, consumers all had alternative suppliers by the time the UN allowed for some production under its Oil-for-Food program. The actual forces most often cited as working behind the high oil prices from 2003 were the relatively rapid growth rates of Gross Domestic Product (GDP) in some developing countries, especially China and India, which led them to greatly increase their oil consumption. It had also been noted that the US dollar declined in value around that time, and as oil prices were set in US dollars on the exchanges, the higher prices were a way of offsetting the weak dollar.

By one account, the weak dollar in 2007 was adding as much as $12–15 per barrel of oil. Other factors included the changing structure of the oil industry, with many megamergers between companies having taken place over the 1990s; OPEC policies of rationing how much oil members put on the market; the rise in gasoline prices independently of oil because of tight refining capacity; the low levels of crude oil stocks; and the shortage of industry equipment, including rigs. Those factors all combined with the usual concerns over political instability in the Middle East as well as Venezuela and Nigeria. Th ere were also concerns about the Russian oil industry, as the Russian oil company Yukos was essentially renationalized in 2006.

In addition, as financial markets were weak, investment portfolios turned to commodities and real estate for profits, and that trading was leading to a speculative drive in its own right. Overall, oil responded to a complex set of circumstances that could not have easily been predicted.

Apart from the financial and demand factors that led to the steep rise in the price of oil after 2002, there were others that were regularly at work.

Those included seasonal swings, as well as natural disasters. Generally, crude oil prices tend to be higher in the winter when demand is larger because of cold weather, and surge again in August when people take to the roads in their cars for vacations and air conditioners are on all day. Prices tend to weaken in the spring with warmer weather. Other factors influencing the price of crude include stockpiling, which occurs in different places at different times.

Ultimately, however, oil prices cannot exceed what people can pay. When prices rise dramatically, a sudden drop in demand is often seen, reflecting an inability to pay the new premiums. Historically that has worked to force the price down again. What was surprising in the first decade of the twenty-first century was that developed countries were able to sustain oil at over $70 per barrel, and it was only after oil topped $100 per barrel that many countries descended into recessions. Th e recessions were blamed on other factors apart from just oil, including poor lending practices on the part of banks and real estate bubbles worldwide.

Although the price of oil dropped precipitously in the second half of 2008, it rebounded over 2009 to the $70s range. Most oil executives felt that was an appropriate level to maintain global production in the region of 85–86 million barrels a day which was the consumption rate at that time, and that the price was in the affordable range for consumers.

The argument that the adjusted post-2008 price was a more accurate reflection of what the true price of oil should be was demonstrated by the attitude of Saudi Arabia towards the price fluctuations. During the period of rising prices from 2003 to 2008, the Saudis—who tend to be conservative over oil prices since their dependency on oil revenues makes them vulnerable to any drop-in demand during recessions—were initially wary of the upward climb in the price of oil and increased their own production to keep the price down.

But by 2005, as there were no signs of a global recession and Organization for Economic Cooperation and Development (OECD) countries were coping with the new prices, the Saudis stepped back from their earlier attempts to keep the price lower and decided it was time to recalibrate their price band. Th at said, many less developed countries had been unable to cope with the high price of oil and had seen their economies negatively affected even before the price hit $50. When prices finally went past an affordable level for the developed states, a drop-in demand was noted in the OECD that was naturally accompanied by a drop-in price. Th e USA, the world's single largest consumer, saw its demand fall from around 22 million barrels a day in 2005 to less than 18.9 million in 2013. By the end of 2009, the price appeared to have been corrected to what was perceived as a realistic level, but political instability in the Middle East in 2011 once again drove prices up. [1]

1.1. Recent Changes in the World Economy and the Global Financial Crisis

In recent years, the modern financial system has become more vulnerable and fragile as a result of complex financial securities, a dependence on short-term funding markets, international trade imbalances, and high corporate and consumer debt levels. Any shock or stimulus, such as the ongoing foreclosure crisis, the failure of key financial institutions, regulatory and market-based controls, or

---

[1]Thijs Van de Graaf • Benjamin K. Sovacool Arunabha Ghosh • Florian Kern • Michael T. Klare: The Palgrave Handbook of the International Political Economy of Energy. 2016. P 230: 233

unhealthy stock and housing markets, could disrupt the delicate equilibrium of the system.

Since late 2008, the subprime mortgage crisis in the United States has spread worldwide. Both developed and developing countries have been adversely affected by the crisis. the world's economic growth rate in 2008 was 1.7 %, a drop of 2.2 % from the previous year, and the growth rate in 2009 was −2.2 %, the lowest since World War II, when growth in the developed countries was −3.3 % and that in the developing countries was 1.2 % (−2.2 % excluding China and India). Global trade decreased by 14.4 % in 2009 and the prices of the major commodities dropped substantially as well. The United States, Japan, European Union, and other developed countries suffered greatly during this Crisis. [1]

The global economic recession and the subsequent quick recovery have brought a great fluctuation in the world's energy prices. The crude oil price for delivery in the New York Commodity Exchange dropped from a record high of 15 USD/barrel on June 3, 2008 to 34 USD/barrel (a drop of 77 %) on December 19, 2008. After March 2009, oil prices started to

---

[1] Yi-Ming Wei • Hua Liao: Energy Economics: Energy Efficiency in China. Springer International Publishing Switzerland 2016. P 12

slowly rise. Generally speaking, the change in oil prices is a quarter earlier than the change in oil developments at the microeconomic level. [1]

Global energy investment fell significantly. global investment in primary oil and gas production decreased by approximately 90 billion USD, with a decrease of 19 %. More than 20 plans for large-scale oil and gas projects (with a daily oil production capacity of approximately 2 million barrels) were cancelled or suspended indefinitely and approximately 29 projects (with a daily oil productive capacity of about 38 thousand barrels) were postponed by at least 18 months. Global investment in bio-energy declined 18 % in 2009. Mergers and acquisitions in the global energy market were also affected by the crisis, but they quickly recovered. mergers and acquisitions of enterprises and assets in terms of primary oil and gas production declined 10.4 billion USD in 2008, a decrease of 50 %, before recovering to 14.5 billion USD in 2009, an increase of 40 %. [2]

---

[1] Yi-Ming Wei • Hua Liao: Energy Economics: Energy Efficiency in China. Springer International Publishing Switzerland 2016. P 12

[2] Yi-Ming Wei • Hua Liao: Energy Economics: Energy Efficiency in China. Springer International Publishing Switzerland 2016. P 14

To face the financial crisis, governments at all levels introduced a series of economic stimulation policies to expand domestic demand, among which the fixed asset investment based on building projects takes a major role in substantially increasing energy demand in 2009. According to measurements and calculations by the World Bank, the year 2009 witnessed the fastest growth in actual investment (18.3 %) since 1993. Due to additional investment, new energy capabilities and ongoing use of private cars, it is estimated that energy demand will continue to be high. [1]

After the first world oil crisis, the developed countries established the International Energy Agency (IEA) to jointly confront the security of the global energy supply. the government budget for energy technology research, development, and demonstration (RD&D) in the countries that participated in the IEA witnessed a rapid increase, rising to $19.1 billion in 1981. Thereafter, following the decline in energy prices, RD&D also declined, slipping to $8.9 billion in 1997. However, in recent years, with the global energy prices soaring and climatic conditions deteriorating, the RD&D budget has experienced another period of tremendous growth, reaching $29.4 billion in

---

[1] Yi-Ming Wei • Hua Liao: Energy Economics: Energy Efficiency in China. Springer International Publishing Switzerland 2016. P 41

2009 (but only returning to the 1981 level, according to PPP). [1]

Assuming that the minimum oil stock level required by the industry to provide the economy with the necessary kinds and amounts of products is 50 days of consumption, and that a 40 % reduction of oil imports occurred, it is possible to determine the number of days the governments could use stocks to maintain a given level of oil consumption. Oil stocks in the 1970s could even out the differences in economic vulnerability among the European countries. This apparently lay behind the production patterns which to some extent existed; some countries (e.g. France, Italy and Japan) maintained higher stock levels, measured against consumption, than others (e.g. Germany). Certainly, by agreeing in advance how they would respond to a supply cut-off, the European governments could greatly reduce the risk that another embargo would result in the type of conflict and strain in their overall relationship which occurred in the 1973–1974 crisis. Moreover, by demonstrating their collective determination to increase their ability to withstand a supply interruption, they could limit the effectiveness of the so-called oil weapon. [2]

---

[1] Yi-Ming Wei • Hua Liao: Energy Economics: Energy Efficiency in China. Springer International Publishing Switzerland 2016. P 286

Estimates of the availability of stocks in Europe varied widely. From the mid-1970s the European Economic Community, the International Energy Agency and various national governments-imposed stock guidelines and requirements on the oil companies, but the definition of stocks differed, and an estimate of how much of those stockpiles could be used without replacement in an emergency was not available. In the initial discussion, both at the IEA and the EEC, it was decided to use the standard OECD definition of stock levels, to deduct from this figure the oil used to fill pipelines and held in various industrial facilities, deduct an additional 10 %, and then call the remainder an "emergency reserve". Later on, it was generally agreed that the IEA definition of "emergency reserve" overstated the amount of oil that could be withdrawn; oil industry managers believed that, as a rule, 40–50 days of oil supplies must be held in stock to allow smooth operation of the distribution system. Thus, the amount of time purchased by oil importers through their stock policies was more limited than a first examination suggested, and once emergency reserves were depleted, there was little the EEC members could do to help one another cope with a large import loss. [1]

([2])Rossella Bardazzi • Maria Grazia Pazienza Alberto Tonini: European Energy and Climate Security. Springer International Publishing Switzerland 2016. P 21

([1])Rossella Bardazzi • Maria Grazia Pazienza Alberto

The reporting period begins with a downward phase, with small deviations from 1995 to 2000. At that time, it meets the fixed point already mentioned: $20/bbl, $20/t, and $2/MMBtu. Then prices begin rising, accompanied by the acceleration of growth, driven by industry in emerging countries and by the debt of Northern countries. Some point to this period as the "super-cycle of raw materials". For energy, the price of oil slowly rises until 2003, before following a rapid rise that led it to the height of $140/bbl in the summer of 2008, right before the fall of Lehman Brothers. Remarkably, the other energies remain in the halo around the price of oil, which means that their relative price, with the quality discount already mentioned, is maintained throughout this period. Only one exception: US natural gas, with at least three price peaks at over $8/MMBtu over this period (2000, 2002, 2005) pushing it from the oil halo. It is during this time that the future shale gas revolution builds up ... After the boom, the economic crisis hits in just a few months. From the summer to winter of 2008, the energy prices pass from level $140-160 ($14-16 for gas) to a level of $40-60 ($4-6 for gas), i.e. a division by three.

Tonini: European Energy and Climate Security. Springer International Publishing Switzerland 2016. P 22: 23

To explore the simultaneous fluctuations in the prices of oil, gas and coal, a "natural price index" can be used: in 2000, the price of oil was $20/bl, coal was $20/t and natural gas was $2/MMBtu. This is really a pure coincidence since the amounts of energy are not the same: a price of $20/bl of oil corresponds to a price per ton of oil equivalent (toe) of $140/toe, $20/t of coal amounts to $30/toe; and finally, $2/MMBtu to $80/toe. The differences in value effectively reflect the hierarchy of energy qualities: in 2000, the value of one energy unit of coal and gas respectively represented 21% and 57% of that of oil. We can thus select the prices of four representative energy products (see the graph below). For oil, an average of three benchmark crudes: West Texas Intermediate, North Sea Brent, and Dubai crude. For natural gas, it is necessary to distinguish the price on the Henry Hub (major gas interconnection in Louisiana) in the United States and the price charged by Russia's Gazprom on the European market. Finally for coal, we consider the export price from South Africa.

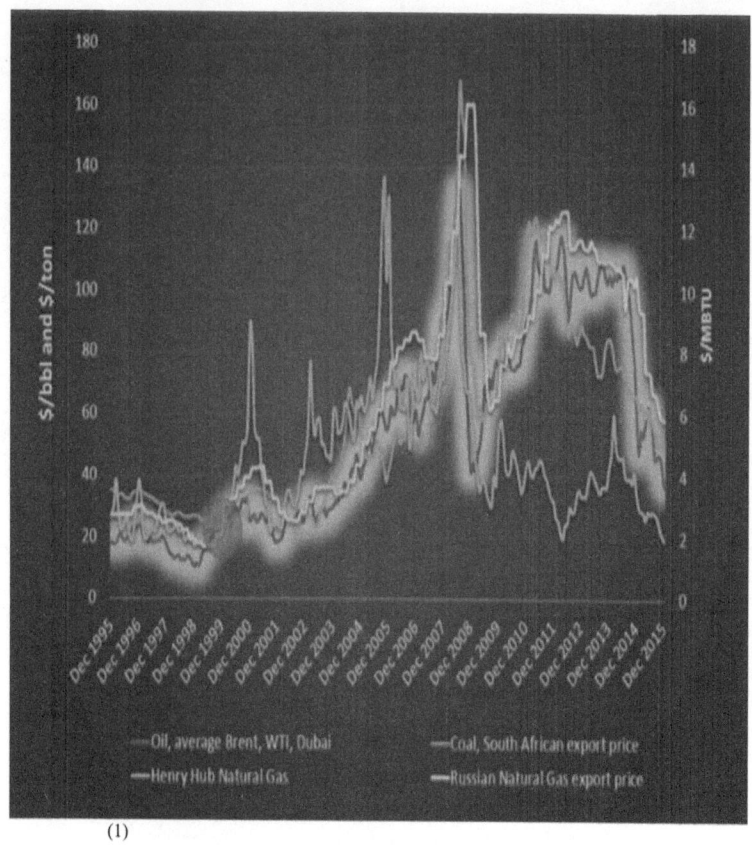
(1)

1.2. The Financial Crisis and Its Impact on the Carbon Price Dynamics

Putting a finger on the exact date when the financial crisis began has proven difficult for both academics and practitioners. Some trace its onset to the Lehman Brothers bankruptcy in

---

[1]enerdata: American (shale) gas, the new benchmark for energy prices?.2016.

September 2008, while others argue it started much earlier in January 2007. We follow prior work in the carbon literature in identifying the start of the financial crisis as the first reduction in interest rates by the U.S. Board of Governors of the Federal Reserve System on 17 August 2007. The dataset is then divided into pre- and full-crisis subsets, covering the periods 22/04/2005 to 16/08/2007 and 17/08/2007 to 30/06/2011, respectively. [1]

Before the start of the crisis, carbon is found to trade on its fundamentals—the energy complex and extreme weather. Oil appears to be the most important driver of carbon prices. The regression coefficients of oil are numerically much larger than the ones for gas: 0.41 (0.23) for intraphase (interphase) EUA futures relative to 0.13 (0.06) for gas. The relationship between the two energy variables and carbon is such that oil and gas price increases are associated with increases in EUA prices. Equity does not seem to affect carbon prices, as demonstrated by the insignificant slope coefficients of the DJ EuroStoxx index. This finding is in line with Bonacina et al. (2009) who argue that before the financial crisis carbon allowances behaved like commodities rather than financial assets. A non-linear relationship between weather and the price

---

[1]Yulia Veld-Merkoulova • Svetlana Viteva: Carbon Finance. Springer International Publishing Switzerland 2016. P 37

of carbon is documented whereby extremely hot and cold days lead to positive abnormal returns (β_{hot} = 0.0125, β_{cold} = 0.0143). Naturally, the significance of extreme temperatures is only limited to the near expiry contracts. [1]

1.3. THE FINANCIAL CRISIS AND THE OIL MARKET

In December 1988, OPEC decided to adopt as reference for the price of crude oil (rather than the value of the Arabian light, the Saudi crude of light quality) the value of the Brent.

At that time, everyone thought that this was the value of the crude produced in the North Sea, the name of which was indeed Brent. No-one realized that this was a misunderstanding, a case of a homonym. The Brent in question was not a crude oil, but a financial commodity.

Let us imagine, for a moment and as a game, which OPEC had decided to adopt, as a reference for fixing the price of oil, the value of a particular type of cherry tomato, to which the creator and biggest producer gave the name of 'Brent'. The reason for the choice could have

---

[1]Yulia Veld-Merkoulova • Svetlana Viteva: Carbon Finance. Springer International Publishing Switzerland 2016. P 55

been the high energy consumption needed to produce the new 'Brent' cherry tomato.

Once the decision was taken, it would become obvious that the price of oil would depend, almost exclusively, on the supply and demand of Brent tomatoes on the international market. A plentiful harvest would equal low prices and a difficult year, high prices. Cherry tomatoes in fashion means high prices; and so on.

No-one would dream of looking, to analyze the movements of the price or to make predictions of the future, at the supply and demand of the physical crude oil.

We have taken the above example as a joke, but one capable, although with the differentiation needed and analyses concerned, of giving us a description that is fairly close to reality. These dynamics of the oil market are slowly beginning to become clear and understandable to the principal subjects in the oil market, producing countries and oil companies.

What is in fact the Brent market, the true one that defines the price of oil? This is a huge game like the 'Panini football stickers', those carrying the picture of football players.

The stickers, once printed and sold, create an exchange market between the children or fans that look for them, and their value varies according to the demand. Those of the famous and popular players will go for more than those of unknown or less well-known players.

Let us imagine that one day, for some reason, the football teams of the world, with the agreement of UEFA and FIFA, decide that the market value of the various players is that of the respective stickers or that they are indexed to that reference.

A double market would be created, that of the football market where against real money a club recruits a player in flesh and blood, and the other where everyone can buy or sell stickers without ever becoming owners of a player. If the market of the stickers should develop massively, thanks to the ease with which it is possible to buy and sell (online for example), it could at a certain point become a form of investment in itself, with participants that have never been interested in football and even less in stickers.

If an international bank, for various reasons, should invest significant amounts of capital in the stickers of a particular player, this would cause an increase in value, regardless of the performance of the player and the policy of the club to which the player belongs.

We would say that the football market has slipped through the hands of the operators of that sport and has become an instrument of financial speculation with positive and negative effects also for the world of football (profits or losses for the bodies that 'own' the players whose stickers are the subject of speculation).

Something similar has taken place in the world of oil. In the eighties a sticker market was created, that of the futures contracts, which is just like plastic cards (or stickers) on which a barrel of crude is depicted.

Whoever buys these plastic cards buys the drawing of a barrel but does not have any possibility of exchanging a plastic card with a real barrel. The market of the oil stickers is a market that is almost totally independent from the real oil market, with bodies operating there and dominating it (controlling it and manipulating it) that normally have no relationship with or interest in the oil industry.

In December 1988, the OPEC countries decided that the price of their crude oils would be fixed on the basis of the value of the 'oil stickers'. This was an almost unnoticed change of a geo-political nature that transferred control and management of the international oil market out of the hands of the OPEC countries into those of the City of London and, slightly less so, Wall Street. This was the event that overturned the balance of the power that had been established since the crisis of 1973.

For years the constant expansion of this parallel market supported the real market. The value of the 'drawing of the barrel' was almost always higher than the one the physical market would have guaranteed, bringing benefits to those who invest in this sector and to the various producing countries. Yes, it is a crazy game, but with a useful purpose.

In the autumn of 2008, the bankruptcy of the principal banks, which owned massive quantities of oil stickers, obliged them to sell the oil stickers and therefore cause a slump in the value of such stickers and hence in the price of oil, the reference value of which derives from these.

From that moment there began talks about the need to review the mechanism used to set the price of oil, but quietly and without haste.

During 2009, the oil price, thanks to the recovery of what we called the sticker market (where the banks have placed a significant share of the money received from the governments), started to increase again.

The attitude of the producing countries became: let us discuss, examine and wait. Any action will eventually be taken if and when the banks find more profitable ways to invest their money, not in the Panini stickers anymore but maybe in the real economy. For now, we carry on this way.

So, we have to resign ourselves to seeing the price of oil go up and down, avoiding having to pretend to be able to explain the correlations between these fluctuations and the fundamentals of the oil industry or the non-existing policies of OPEC.

For most of 2009 and 2010, we saw the price fluctuating, in the range of $70–80 per barrel. Everybody started to announce the new kind of ideal range of the price of oil, considered sacred by the main OPEC official representatives. As usual the market, a few months later, deviated from all these guidelines given by the gurus and by the authorities. We can say, then, that since December 1988 the global reference for the price of crude has lost its direct relationship with the physical market.

Initially, the oil futures market had in common with the oil market, apart from the name Brent, the historic fact that it was born to support the trading operations of the oil companies, as a financial instrument to provide risk hedging against oscillations in crude oil prices.

At the start of the year 2000, the oil futures market detached itself almost completely from its original nature, becoming a market purely for financial purposes. International banks entered this business without having any involment in the oil business, just as an opportunity to make profit, but some oil companies and almost all the oil trading organizations also started to consider the futures market as an independent business beyond the hedging purposes. All those analysts who tried to explain the movements of the crude oil price on the basis of the evolution of the relationship between demand and supply of physical crude have failed, simply because the link between the financial market and the crude oil market has become increasing ephemeral or even non-existent.

The graph in the Figure clearly shows how the volume of business on the crude oil futures market has risen tenfold in the last 10 years, closely following the entry of the great financial institutions in this field and the change in the attitude of the traditional oil players. This has caused the complete disruption of the internal dynamics of the oil market.

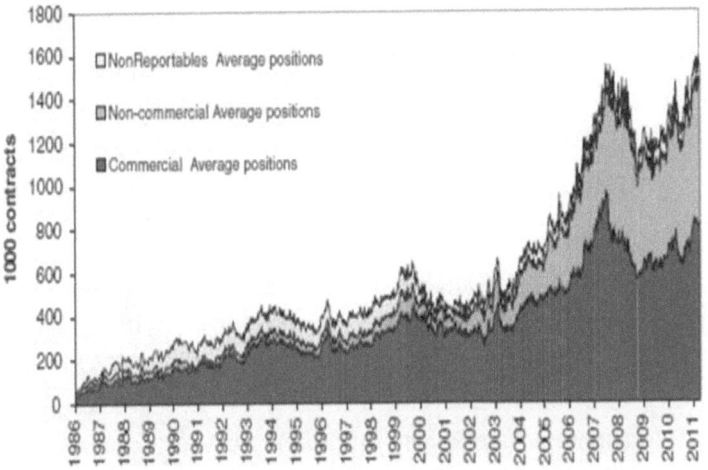

Brent (on paper, financial) is now traded on the market simply for investment purposes or financial speculation, to protect capital by parking it in a safe place for a certain period of time (even just for a few minutes), to profit from a momentary wave of speculation, or to manipulate a market which otherwise would be stable.

To understand better the size of the phenomenon, let us glance at the numbers of this business, which is almost unknown to those who complain about the price of gasoline.

During 2008–2010, with world crude production around 86 million barrels per day, only about 20 million barrels per day were marketed.

The remainder, about 65 million barrels per day, was not put on the international markets because it was consumed directly by the producing countries.

If we refer to a valuation made in the period January 2008–December 2010, with an average price for Brent of $80 per barrel, we can easily calculate that the value of the mass of money in movement due to purchases and sales of physical crude as traded amounts to around $1,900 billion.

If we further assume that all the crude produced (86 million barrels per day) was traded at market price, the mass of money in play, in the same period from January 2008 to December 2010, would have been around $7,600 billion. The balance between demand and supply of physical crude at world level fluctuates within these values.

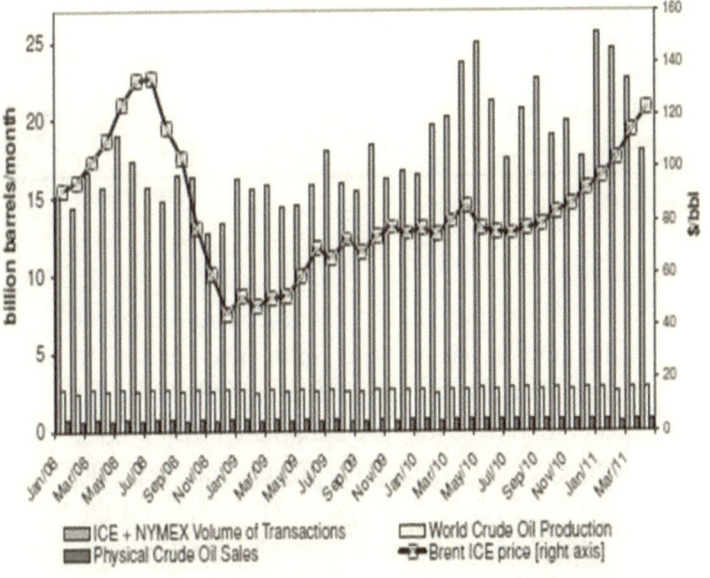

In theory the futures market for Brent was created to stabilize crude prices after the epic oil crises of the 1970s and 1980s. The daily quotation for Brent was supposed to permit greater transparency in the transactions and thus a stabilization of prices in the short and medium term. In the early years this was the case; the volumes of crude traded on the futures

	January 2008–December 2010				
	Production of Physical Crude Oil	Transactions of Physical Crude Oil	Transaction of equivalent oil in the financial market	Ratio Futures/ Physical	Ratio Physical/ Futures
Volume (billion barrels)	93.7	23.4	623.1	27	3.8%
Value (billion $)	7,594	1,899	50,806	27	3.7%

Sources: NYMEX and International Energy Agency

market never exceeded the physical quantities produced and sold. This can only mean that the oil companies operated on the paper market to stabilize the price of their crudes with hedging operations. Today we see 580 million barrels of oil equivalent arriving on the market – which strangely enough we continue to call an oil market – and they are behind the real dynamics that move the quotation for Brent, which is still called, for no good reason, the price of crude oil. [1]

1.4. The Costs of the First Oil Shock

For a long time, the choice among alternative technologies was effectively limited to coal-nuclear options. Taking into consideration, the course of events during the

---

[1] Salvatore Carollo: Understanding Oil Prices A John Wiley & Sons, Ltd., Publication. 2012. P 10:16

heroic years of European reconstruction, marked by chronic energy shortages, one might expect the blossoming of power stations equipped with fuel–oil boilers.

However, in effect, the swift adoption of oil as a source of electric power proved to be a false start. In Great Britain and especially in France, fuel–oil receded into the background after the nationalization of the Suez Canal by Egyptian president Nasser on July 26, 1956, and the ensuing invasion of the canal zone by British, French, and Israeli troops. During the conflict and its aftermath, the canal was closed to commercial shipping and the Levant pipelines, carrying oil from Saudi Arabia to the Mediterranean, were also shutdown, causing wide-ranging disruptions to three quarters of European supplies. The last quarter of 1956 and the first months of 1957 witnessed a governmental nightmare, with rationing of motor fuels and rationing electricity supply to both domestic households and to companies and manufacturers. The return to normality left a sense of trauma as regards the way the security of energy supplies had hitherto been planned and designed, with "caution" as the watchword to be stressed into the future. Dependence on Middle East oil required solutions and European governments steadfastly decided to resume the installation of oil-burning equipment and step up investment in nuclear power stations.

Revealingly, the orientation of governments did not change greatly when oil prices dropped to all-time lows in the 1960s. The Suez memory still remained fresh and ministers resisted pressures from the electrical utilities to generate power resorting to highly competitive fuel–oil imports. Moreover, the defense of a moderate and controlled rundown of the industrial workforce at coal mines was also at stake. In Great Britain, two oil-fired stations were authorized (Fawley and Pembroke) but the first Labor government of Harold Wilson refused consent for the installation of a third oil-fired station at Little brook D and issued a virtual ban on conversions from coal to oil in the Fuel Policy White Paper released in 1967. The Central Electricity Generation Board—CEGB, however, continued its unyielding pressure and did not allow the issue to lapse as oil-firing power stations displayed the lowest levelized costs of all classical thermal stations, presented the highest thermal efficiency and provided twice the average calorific value of coal per unit of weight. Ultimately, labor had to give up some conversions. In France, some oil-firing stations (mostly dual firing, which meant that they were switchable between oil and coal over a 15-day schedule) were authorized, albeit with only a limited weighting in the overall energy system.

After a decade of caution and compromise, the switch to fuel–oil quickened significantly in 1970. In just four months, about 3,250 MW of coal-firing stations, involving a total of 30 boilers, were converted in Great Britain to either oil or natural gas-firing while France experienced the same process one year later with the adaptation of 1,750 MW, plus another 1,000 MW, to fuel–oil burning. With this alteration, the technological plateau of 250 MW power stations was switched from coal to oil in France. The trend proceeded apace in the ensuing years, backed up by long-term contracts signed with the oil business giants: BP, Shell-Mex, Esso and Texaco (then called the "Regent"), on the one hand, and Elf-Aquitaine (*Union Générale des Pétroles*) on the other. On the eve of 1974, 39 % of the electricity produced by *Electricité de France–EDF* and 22 % of the electricity produced by the Central Electricity Generating Board–CEGB was generated by oil-firing stations.

Inasmuch as levelized costs demonstrated that oil-firing was cheaper outside of base load periods, it became increasingly difficult to justify political bans couched in arguments of coal protection, strategic security of supply, or balance of payments stability. In this respect, the 1970 turning point indicates that the equilibrium of powers had tilted definitely in favor of the electricity utilities. Many reasons seemed to have accrued to this turnaround: Growing concerns over air pollution and the fact that fuel–oil power stations released less grit, dust, and CO2 than coal stations; the expansion of national refinery capacities and the ensuing local availability of larger quantities of fuel–oil, along with the boost to demand for gasoline; full-on optimism linked to the hot technological revolution thinking surrounding British North Sea gas and oil; the bridging role played in France by Pierre Guillaumat, simultaneously the head of EDF and of the major French oil company. On the other hand, the conjuncture proved not just favorable to oil-firing but also adverse to its competing technologies: There was widespread uncertainty over the technological paths for the future development of nuclear power with a deadlock between graphite gas and pressurized water reactors; the expectations of forthcoming coal shortages prevailing over the course of the winters of 1970 and 1971; a decrease in productivity of coal mining; mounting doubts around the rationality of energy investments voiced by the treasuries of both countries.

Nevertheless, within this mix of structure and action, the pivotal driver of change toward electricity fuelization seems to have derived more from the side of action.

However, important the aforementioned factors might have been, what actually triggered the swift fuelization was the restatement that state-owned enterprises should be judged by their commercial success. In practice, and not just in theory, governments accepted the independence of public boards. This policy of public sector competitiveness involved an overture to foreign competition, technological modernization and support for a policy of "national champions" was put into practice in the final phase of the British Labour government of Harold Wilson (1964– 1970) and pressed ahead with, but not without problems, by the Conservative administration of Edward Heath (1970–1974). In France, such a strategy was pursued during George Pompidou's presidency in a retreat from the previous Gaullist orientation. As a consequence of the liberal-commercial approach, the electricity utilities expanded their freedom of choice between technologies, between fuels, and between investments.

When free to choose oil-firing, they grabbed at the opportunity. Most of the concerns over the security of oil supplies seemed to vanish at the beginning of the 1970s. As always, individuals foresaw the future as a variation of known patterns—in an echo that reverberated with ever less amplitude. These mindsets led Western decision-makers to spotlight core events in oil-producing countries. To European eyes, the crux of matter lay in the changeover in Libya where the newly arrived leader Muammar al Qaddafi compelled the western concessionaire companies to concede higher taxes and higher prices to the government, under the mantle of anti-Zionism and anti-imperialism. After that, the common agreement established at the Teheran and Tripoli conferences by the OPEC member states spread the benefits of the Libyan example far further, forcing the oil majors to concede much higher host-government "takes." These developments drove oil price increases: The posted price in the Middle East rose from $1.80 to $3.00 per barrel between 1970 and 1973.

Looking at the reports and the scenarios predicted at the time by French and British analysts, one nevertheless gets the sensation that they tended to understate the risks associated with both the political as well as with the market conjuncture.

Within the respective ministries of industry and power as well as the electrical utilities, the experts consistently agreed that there were a "number of factors likely to restrain OPEC members from pushing claims for increased prices to extremes," or that the "tax yield of oil-producing nations will tend to diminish (at least marginally for the extraction of crude exceeding the normal extraction plans)

….." This very same view was aired by energy expert "gurus" like Maurice Adelman or Paul Frankel. On the geostrategic level, one finds the very same underestimation, if not outright disregard, about what was going on in the Middle East in the high-ranking decision-making spheres of the US administration where President Richard Nixon apparently seemed more alarmed over the emerging Watergate case scandal.

Within this context, all that might reasonably be expected were minor and incremental increases in the price of Middle Eastern crude since the market and bargaining position of Arab countries had been exhausted. It was then believed that the upper hand now belonged to the West and the petroleum-based electricity generators would bask in a glow of growth and development. More troublesome were perhaps the long-term prospects. Should consumption continue to mount and the level of reserves not be supplemented by new discoveries, the threat of impending depletion had to be taken seriously. Although this sort of expert wariness was not imbued with the critique of technological optimism that pervaded some ecological thinking (for instance the "Limits to growth" report released in 1973), it nonetheless anticipated the enhanced scarcity would reflect in higher prices: In the approximate forthcoming 15 years, a shortage premium would thus push prices upward. The levelized cost forecasts of oil-firing power stations therefore envisaged stability in the cost of crude, perhaps with certain marginal increases over the period 1973–1985, followed by a rising trend there afterward.

Such a future, however, represented a variation of the already identified patterns. The oil embargo thus came as a complete surprise. On October 17, 1973, 11 days after the outbreak of the Egyptian–Israeli war, Arab oil ministers meeting in Kuwait agreed to institute a total oil embargo against the United States and other countries friendly to Israel. Additionally, they decided to cut back production by 5 % from the September level and to continue cutting by 5 % in each succeeding month until their objectives were met. The ensuing escalation drove oil prices to the unprecedented level of $11.65 per barrel.

The "oil shock" concept encapsulates the psychological sense of perplexity alongside the rippling effects felt throughout the entire extent of the economy. Furthermore, the disturbances in the oil market were no short-lived phenomenon but were bound up with the turnover generated throughout the business cycles and impacting on inflation, wage-price spirals, rising interest rates, falling investment, increasing unemployment, decreasing productivity, and long-term decreases in economic growth. The "first oil shock" therefore refers to the sequence of events that spans the Kuwait embargo declaration in October 1973 right through to October 1978, when a second shock rippled through the system (Iranian oil workers walking out on strike at the outbreak of the Iran–Iraq war).

In response to higher energy prices, firms and households tend to consume less energy while enterprises making recourse to energy-intensive capital stocks may experience a faster depreciation of their stocks. In addition, the cost structure changed in explosive and erratic ways, owing to the drag effects of oil upon coal prices combined with an upswing in the price trend for natural uranium, which first began rising in 1972. Equally, the consequences of inflation upon equipment, facilities, and workforce remuneration were hard to grasp, let alone to forecast.

For over 25 years, experts had mostly focused on capital cost-related issues. More to the point, they tried to ascertain the sensitivity of costs to modifications in upscaling. Tactically, it was assumed that other factors in the levelized cost formula remained to a greater or lesser extent stable. Now, in the midst of the 1973 upheaval everything in the formula seemed to change overnight: capital costs and fuel costs as well as operational and maintenance costs. Without a past anchor to form the foundation, it proved really hard to convey an accurate picture of the best future choices. Yet, at no other stage was such information more urgently needed. Public utility policymakers and managers turned their attention to altering the energy mix and shifting the balance away from petroleum. This was furthermore crucial because the most recent equipment commissioned by France and Great Britain was for oil-firing power stations and flexible dual firing to allow for a quick switchover between oil and coal. However, it remained to be ascertained not only just which technology was more competitive but also the most appropriate energy mix.

The Figure represents the levelized costs of electricity generation for coal, oil, and nuclear power stations in Great Britain and France. The gross domestic product deflator was applied to account for nominal costs and express all values in constant 1978 prices. The data were compiled from historical archives and printed sources, in particular, the reports and accounts issued by the electricity utilities. Each graph discloses the prospective levelized costs and thus the cost of the last power station either commissioned or constructed for each respective technology in use. Insofar as any decision is undertaken at a specific point in time, this is the most relevant data that historical actors seek out, simply because it represents the most updated information available

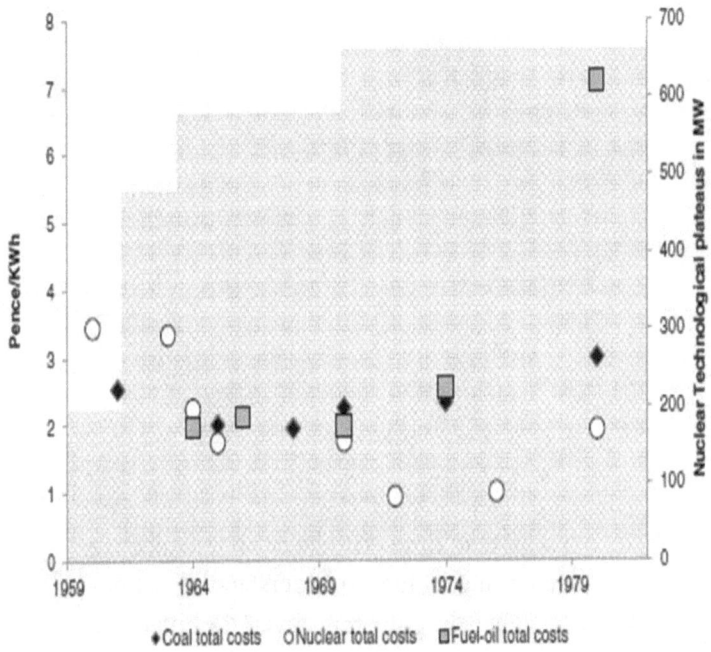

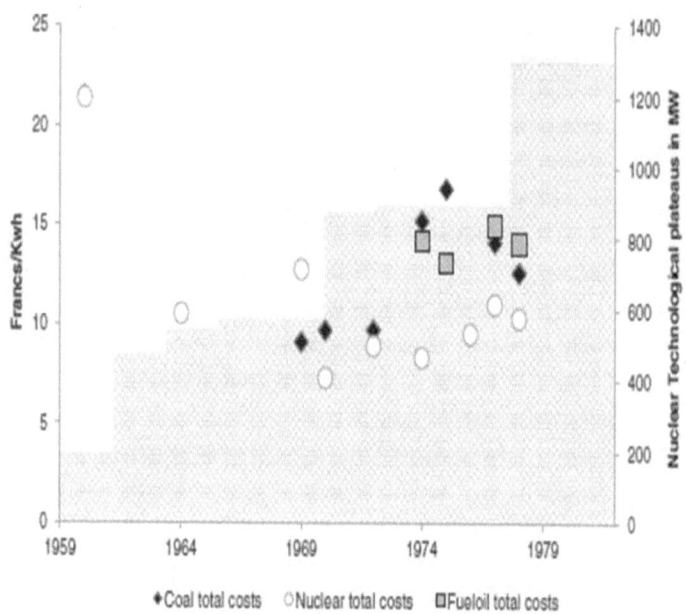

♦Coal total costs　ONuclear total costs　☐Fueloil total costs

at that time. However, if prospective costs are pertinent clues to understanding actions and decisions, they do not cover the total real cost. More often than not, several contingencies occurring during the siting, construction, and/or test phases add further costs to the overall project. For this reason, the results depicted in the Fig. do not capture the final accounts signed off for the project but rather the conditional evidence upon which the decisions were actually grounded. Finally, the upscaling trend in the evolution of nuclear power's technological plateau is shown in the gray background area of the Fig. and represented along the right vertical axis.

As all values are expressed in constant 1978 costs, the slope of the downward cost trend since the 1950s reveals the pace of technological progress, economies of scale, and standardization. As previously stated, by the close of the 1960s, this descendent trajectory flattened out. Herewith nuclear costs appear positioned below oil and below coal, indicating the expectations of a breakthrough in atomic energy power costs per KWh. According to the perspective of the historical actors depicted by the graph, two events took place in the aftermath of the 1973–1974 crisis: First, there is the inversion in the overall cycle, ushering in an age of high energy prices; second, the investment prospects for nuclear power become increasingly bright while, further distant in the appraisal, oil and coal exchange relative positions, with petroleum relegated to an uncompetitive ranking.

Although both nations presented similar orderings of their options, the fact is that French levelized costs looked clearly sharper cut in real terms and displaying larger divergences between the respective life cycle costs of nuclear, coal, and oil stations. From here, it logically follows that the pressure to change the energy mix so as to take advantage of forthright differences in costs appears greater on the French side. The turn of events confirmed this outlook. When the oil crisis hit in 1973, already looming on the French horizon was an ambitious program based on the adaptation of the original Westinghouse-licensed 900 MW pressurized water nuclear reactor design along with a European partnership for the installation of uranium enrichment plant (to be located in *Tricasin*, in the *Rhone-Alpes* region).

With the national resource base of competitive coal dwindling year by year, Prime Minister Pierre Messmer moved resolutely to announce a countervailing strategy based on the ordering of 13,000 MW reactors within just two years. The ensuing government headed by Valery Giscard D'Estaing not only confirmed this bet on nuclear but even amplified the vision of French energy independence and security through pro-active policies in the domain of transportation, energy conservation, and energy diplomacy. Unfortunately, not everything ran quite as expected and EDF and the Giscard government soon came across enhanced delays in construction and thus accruing additional interest and other escalations in nuclear power investment costs. Despite these burdensome circumstances, there was no retrenchment in the civil atomic program. The momentous turmoil of 1973 embodied the take-off of France as the world leader in nuclear energy and turning it into the country that currently generates the largest percentage share of nuclear electricity alongside Lithuania.

Nothing similar occurred in Great Britain. To put it simply, aside from the sharp attention to the boost in oil consumption and the concessions of North Sea oil fields and aside from their immediate exploitation through the installation of 70 MW sets of gas turbines, little seemed to change in British energy policy. There were some measures aimed at promoting energy conservation which attracted some public discussion but what is hard to find is either the kind of event-reaction sequence or the sense of urgency experienced by the French. Partly, this stemmed from the fact that Britain had itself become an oil producer and with perfect timing given the upward trend in prices which allowed the country to bypass the issues of supply security that beset other nations. Partly, this also resulted from the Labor government of Harold Wilson and his charismatic Secretary of State for Energy Tony Benn being far too occupied in fighting the fires then bursting out all around: wage demands, business failures, European integration, curtailing inflation, and the collapse of sterling. However, the single most important reason was that the British energy system experienced excess capacity in terms of electricity generation and had consequently fewer degrees of freedom to alter the energy mix: from the 5,500 MW new power generators commissioned at the 1972 peak, the system went into steep decline until a minimum of 57 MW, commissioned in 1978. The slowing of energy consumption brought about by the oil shock further aggravated the braking of investments. Likewise, three of the four new nuclear stations under construction in 1973–1974 were plagued with technical problems and recursive delays amplifying naturally amplifying the misgivings about the real levelized costs of nuclear power. Changes were therefore correspondingly slow and no grand plan saw the light of day. Over time, natural gas and imported coal fulfilled a much larger role in the electricity system transforming Britain into a balanced "four-fuel" economy: gas, coal, nuclear, and oil.

The previous chapters suggest that economic engineering formulas, such as that of levelized costs, may be approached from different angles. Whereas in periods of relative price stability, all concerns centered on improvements that may prompt reductions in capital costs, in periods of higher volatility, particularly when affecting fuel prices, the focus switches to trend forecasting and the implementation of energy-saving procedures. Depending on the historical circumstances, the same formula may be viewed through the lens of "yesterday's costs"—the most updated estimates of existing equipment and installations—or through the lens of "tomorrow costs"—the likely evolution of fuels prices. When the present is deeply ingrained into the past, technology deserves much closer attention; when the present depends on the future, markets become much more important.

In any case, the levelized accounting cost methodology bears a clear resemblance to Bayesian probabilities in the sense that all hypotheses are based on conditional evidence and subject to review whenever new evidence is produced. [1]

The role of the 1973–74 oil crisis is pivotal in revealing the tip of decartelization and subsequent globalization of oil. This includes the illustration of an evolutionary mechanism that includes competitive worldwide pricing of oil against unequal costs (and productivities) of the various oil-producing regions. As is demonstrated, the crisis indeed has led to decartelization of oil in all oil regions of the world— including US oil and at the same time, through Organization of the Petroleum Exporting Countries (OPEC) (as a competitive context in spot and future markets for all oil irrespective of geographical location).

[1] Nuno Luis Madureira: Key Concepts in Energy. Springer International Publishing Switzerland 2014. P 203: 210

The kernel of confusion on the question of oil is not the difference in conceptualization between the Right and the Left. It is rather the similitude of imagination that makes them party to the spread of misinformation and cover-up on the alleged causal relation of oil and war in the present era. It shall be demonstrated that, by imitating the right-wing notion of competition and its idealist (i.e., axiomatic) spectrum of pure competition/pure monopoly, the liberal/radical Left succumbs to a nostalgic theory that still describes the present according to the past history under the aegis of cartelized oil. [1]

The oil crisis of 1973–74 was the symptom of the underlying fundamental changes that forcefully led to the internationalization of the oil industry. The production and pricing of crude oil associated with the various oil-producing regions of the world have since become part of a unified process through global competition. It was a mother of all crises that led to the restructuring of all oil, thus brought cheap and not so cheap oil under one all-inclusive, globalized market.

This prompted the collapse of the International Petroleum Cartel (1928–72); this

---

[1] Cyrus Bina: A Prelude to the Foundation of Political Economy. PALGRAVE MACMILLAN. 2013. P 5

included the intricate basing-point pricing system at the Gulf of Mexico and the Persian Gulf, and what lingered as the institutional wherewithal and purposeful paraphernalia linked to the cartel's success. In the meantime, the "Postwar Petroleum Order"—an indispensable part of the international order of the Pax Americana (1945–79)—had begun to fall by the wayside, and the umbilical cord of the US foreign policy was cut from cartelized oil for good. The crisis appeared as a faint signal at first. This prompted the United States and its habitual Western alliance, and the titans of the International Petroleum Cartel (IPC), to engage in an old mode of diplomacy and negotiation to find a customary solution. But it soon became clear that not only the Middle East oil but all oil across the world had also crossed the Rubicon— the new era was about to begin. A cauldron that had been bubbling for quite a while—perhaps since the days of nationalization of oil in Iran and the overthrow of Mohammad Mossadegh— blew its top like a gigantic volcano. The steely law of history seemed to have shown an ironic display of objectivity and resolve. The gusher of discontent was so vast, so dense, and so sudden that it took years to sink in even in the psyche of regulars who thought they had intimate knowledge of oil and politics.

And, while bewildered or struck by a healthy bolt of amnesia, the vast majority to this date is still underestimating.

In contrast to the prevailing opinions at the time, the significance of the oil crisis was not due to the (temporary) shortage that resulted from the imposition of the embargo; rather, the oil embargo itself was the symptom that revealed an underlying transition that had already been taking place toward the globalization of the oil industry.

One has to appreciate that the process of structural transformation in oil production had already begun in the late 1960s and early 1970s. The 1973 oil crisis was simply the culmination of that process, which ushered in an entirely new period in which an end was put to separate regional pricing, inadequate unification, and localized value formation within the global structure. The oil crisis of 1973–74 was not an ordinary oil shortage, similar to the ones that the world experienced in the 1956 Suez Crisis or the 1967 Arab- Israeli clash. This crisis was conveyed by a severe shortage resulting from the Arab oil embargo (see Akins 1973), but it was underpinned by socioeconomic/sociopolitical forces that had long been laid at work toward the persistent transformation of global order.

Hence it would be naive to reduce the oil crisis of the early 1970s to its manifold effects and multifarious impacts such as the suddenness of supply interruption and shortage alone. In the wake of the crisis stood the restructuring of the entire oil sector from top to bottom, doing away with monopoly and allowing price determination through global competition—including competition between the least and the most productive oil regions of the world. These conditions, in turn, necessitated the formation of market prices that were based upon production costs of the least productive oil region, and the synchronized formation of differential oil rents in step with the existing productivity of oil fields across the various oil regions of the globe.

We shall demonstrate that the formation of differential oil rent came about through increased competitive conditions rather than through monopoly. We shall identify the US oil region as the least productive in the world and show that during the period leading up to the crisis there was a significant decline in the productivity of the aging US oil fields. The increase in the cost of production of the least productive oil region together with the internationalization of oil production, led to the generalization of high market prices within the entire industry.

The first section is a critical review of the literature on the oil crisis. The second section examines the characteristic features of US oil production. The third section presents an alternative theory of the oil crisis. The chapter concludes with a summation and setting the crisis within a larger polity. [1]

1.5. Monetary Policy

After the subprime mortgage crisis, the weak exchange rate of the dollar caused by the country's quantitative easing, pushed oil prices in dollars upward from 2009 to 2012 by causing investors to invest in the oil market and other commodity markets while the world economy was in recession. As a result, large amounts of capital entered the crude oil market as investors found it safer than capital markets, which had collapsed. Because of this new demand, oil prices started to rise sharply in 2009, when the US and many other economies were in recession. This trend had the effect of imposing a longer recovery time on the global economy, as oil has been shown to be one of the most important production inputs.

Now, let's move to the end of 2014 to see what has happened more recently. In 2014, financial conditions eased compared to 2013. In

[1] Cyrus Bina: A Prelude to the Foundation of Political Economy. PALGRAVE MACMILLAN. 2013. P 17:19

particular, long-term interest rates have declined in developed economies because of the economic recovery and expectations of a lower neutral policy rate in the US over the medium term.

Equity prices have risen and risk premiums declined in developed economies and emerging markets. In the US, both the Dow Jones Industrial Average (Dow) and the S&P 500 powered to record highs, boosted by the strengthening US economy and liquidity provided by the Federal Reserve's unprecedented quantitative easing. The Dow, surpassed two key psychological levels during 2014—17,000 and 18,000—and the S&P 500, also surpassed the 2,000 milestones.

This means that the liquidity mainly provided by the Federal Reserve, especially during the 2008–2009 global financial crisis, transferred to the oil market and created a large demand causing a surge in oil prices in early 2009. Now, because the US and some other developed and emerging capital markets are recovering, it has moved back to the capital markets. This is the reason for the reduced global oil demand, which resulted in the price collapse in the market. This means that this factor may have played a stronger role than supply and lower economic growth. [1]

A descriptive analysis of crude oil markets enables us to observe oil price movements during two sub-periods: 1960–1980 and 1980–2011. The initial period of 1960–1980 witnessed a series of oil price shocks in which price hikes culminated in 1980 at a price of $36.83 per barrel in nominal terms from $1.90 per barrel in 1960. Figure illustrates crude oil price movements in nominal and real terms between 1960 and 2011.

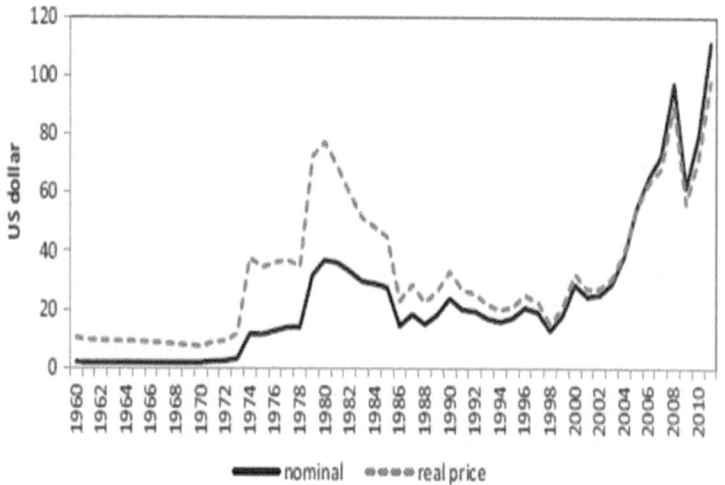

―――――――――――――――――――――――

([1])Naoyuki Yoshino • Farhad Taghizadeh-Hesary: Monetary Policy and the Oil Market. Asian Development Bank Institute 2016. P 4

The production of crude oil increased during the first period (1960–1980) at an average rate of 4.95 %, moving to a production rate of 59.4 million barrels per day (mbd) in 1980 from 21 mbd in 1960. In contrast to the stable crude oil output growth before 1973, the first oil price shock in 1973 initiated recurrent changes in oil production and a dissociation between the Organization of the Petroleum Exporting Countries (OPEC) and non-OPEC output. Figure shows the remarkable contrast in the behavior of OPEC and non-OPEC production in the period after the first oil price shock until 1985. From 1985 to 2011, however, both OPEC and non-OPEC output moved almost steadily parallel to each other. Figure shows the growth rate of OPEC and global crude oil output.

During the second sub-period of 1980–2011, in the early 1980s a recession reduced crude oil demand and exerted significant downward pressure on oil prices.

By the end of the decade, prices had declined substantially to below $25 per barrel. The Persian Gulf War (1990–1991) had an impact on supply and prices as well.

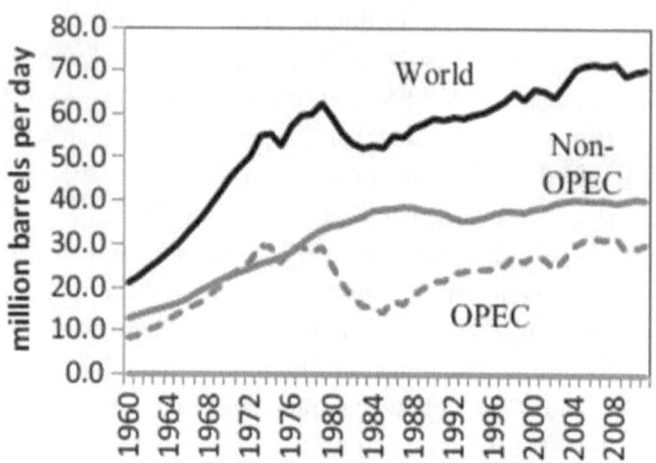

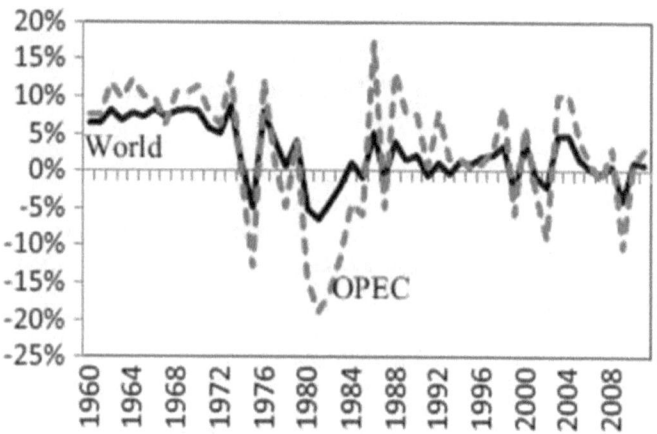

Despite the low prices for crude oil for most of the 1990s, there was little interest within OPEC to try to raise prices. This lack of action by OPEC kept oil prices low for an extended period. However, when crude oil prices descended to $10 per barrel following the Asian financial crisis in 1998, OPEC instituted a series of production cuts starting in late 1999, making it possible for them to raise oil prices. During 1980–2011, average oil prices saw an extreme rise, from about $36 per barrel in 1981 to beyond $111 per barrel in 2011. At the same time, average interest rates devalued from 16.7 % annually in 1981 to about 0.1 % annually in 2011. We explain this long-term price increase, especially after the year 2000, to be caused by expansionary monetary policies that led to lower interest rates, amplified both credit and aggregate demand, and expanded demand for oil, leading to elevated oil prices. Bernanke et al. (1997) stated that the Federal Reserve tends to raise interest rates too high in response to high oil prices, which can lead to depressed economic activity that exceeds the negative effects of oil price shocks. In short, they showed that expansionary monetary policies could have largely eliminated the negative output consequences of the oil-price shocks on the United States (US) economy. Hamilton and Herrera (2004) challenged this view and argue that Bernanke's, Gertler's, and Watson's (BGW) empirical results are driven by model misspecification. Hamilton and Herrera reproduce the BGW experiment using a different model specification and found that increases in the price of oil lead directly to contractions in real output. Tightening monetary policy plays only a secondary role in generating the downturn.

There are several other recent research studies that critically reevaluate the results in Bernanke et al. (1997). For example, Leduc's and Sill's (2014) findings approximated the US Federal Reserve's behavior since 1979, showing that the monetary policy contributes to an approximate 40 % drop in output following a rise in oil prices. Kormilitsina (2011) used an estimated dynamic stochastic general equilibrium model with the demand for oil to contrast the Ramsey optimal with estimated monetary policy. The study found that monetary policy amplified the negative effect of the oil price shock. Or in a more recent study, Yoshino and Taghizadeh-Hesary (2014) examine how monetary policy affected crude oil prices after the subprime mortgage crisis. They found that after the crisis the weaker exchange rate of the dollar caused by the country's quantitative easing pushed oil prices in dollars upward in 2009 causing investors to invest in the oil market and other commodity markets while the world economy was in recession in this period.

This trend had the effect of imposing a longer recovery time on the global economy, as oil has been shown to be one of the most important production inputs. monetary policy indeed has negative effects on the demand side of the crude oil market and, subsequently, on oil prices. We argue that global oil demand was significantly influenced by interest rates. Our research indicates that aggressive monetary policy stimulates oil demand. This demand however, is met with rigid oil supply, creating inflationary trends and disrupting economic growth.

In the last section of this research, we attempted to shed light on the hypothesis of equilibrium vs. disequilibrium in the oil market; our results showed that oil prices adjust instantly, indicating the existence of equilibrium in the oil market during 1960–2011. [1]

1.6. Secular Stagnation

From 1965 to 2015 the world economy, and its energy use, increased substantially even while some countries appeared to be getting more efficient. But the growth of most of the world's industrialized economies have declined enormously in recent years. As of mid-2016 the GDP of countries in Europe and Japan had been essentially stagnant for a decade or two. The United States had a GDP growth rate of 1.1 %, extremely low by

---

[1] Naoyuki Yoshino • Farhad Taghizadeh-Hesary: Monetary Policy and the Oil Market. Asian Development Bank Institute 2016. P 7: 10

historical standards and about the same as the population growth—hence no average increase in per capita wealth. Amongst economists there is considerable discussion and controversy about this (e.g., Galbraith 2014; Irwin 2016). Much of this focuses on factors internal to the economy: consumer spending, debt, banks, deficit spending and Keynesianism—whether or why governmental deficit spending, which has been used extensively in the past to "jump start" economic growth, no longer works as it once did. There is nothing consistent in conventional economics that has an explanation for this general secular stagnation. It is possible that a new approach to economics called BioPhysical Economics, which attempts to make economics based on the natural sciences rather than the social science-based discipline that it is, may provide such explanation. Most adherents to biophysical economics believe (as do many others) that conventional (neoclassical) economics is fundamentally flawed. According to Hall et al. (2001) conventional economics cannot possibly be accepted by people trained in the natural sciences because: [1]

(1) its basic model violates the laws of thermodynamics

---

[1] Charles A.S. Hall: Energy Return on Investment. 2017. P 159

(2) the boundaries used for analysis are incorrect and

(3) its basic premises are put forth as givens rather than tested hypotheses.

The Organization of the Petroleum Exporting Countries (OPEC) exerted its power over the oil supply to punish the West as a consequence of the Yom Kippur War.

The Iran hostage crisis in 1979 further disrupted oil supplies from the Middle East. The response by the USA during the oil crisis was to move quickly toward conservation.

The USA established the strategic petroleum reserve, rationed gasoline, lowered speed limits, and established fuel efficiency standards—Corporate Average Fuel Economy (CAFE) Standards—for automobiles. In the first 6 years of the 1980s, the inflation-adjusted value of oil dropped precipitously due to these conservation efforts, the easing of geopolitical tensions, and, in the latter part of those 6 years, a price war among OPEC nations and an increase in non-OPEC oil production.

It thereafter stabilized at US$ 10–30 per barrel in inflation-adjusted dollars (2006 base year), the secular price of oil in the post-WWII era. The typical time series price display for oil was a series of spiked prices around this trend.

The stabilized secular price thwarted further efforts toward conservation and thermodynamic efficiency that were begun in the 1970s. Jonathan Harris stated, "The availability of cheap energy creates an economic incentive to shift toward energy-intensive production methods. Rather than conserving energy, which would be thermodynamically efficient, low prices encourage individuals and firms to substitute energy for labor and capital." This thereby undercut the thermodynamic efficiency of production per barrel of oil. As early as 1981, the leaders of OPEC clearly understood the implications for oil demand should conservation efforts and thermodynamic efficiency continue. In 1981, Saudi Arabia's oil minister was quoted as stating, "If we force Western countries to invest heavily in finding alternative sources of energy, they will.... This will take them no more than seven to 10 years and will result in their reduced dependence on oil as a source of energy to a point which will jeopardize Saudi Arabia's interests". The stability of the secular price of oil was maintained until the early twenty-first century.

Since 2002, dollar prices of oil have oscillated dramatically. They went from US$ 20 a barrel to nearly US$ 150 by midsummer 2008. The dramatic upward trend was fueled, in part, by speculation run amok, geopolitical uncertainty and chaos, and the rapid economic growth in China and India. In 2009, amidst a deepening recession and collapse of the financial markets, the price temporarily dropped to the low US$ 40, but since has increased to nearly US$ 100 a barrel. The downward movement was coincident with demand destruction; that is, the downward trend in the use of oil due to high prices and a recession. Despite the fact that the global economic recovery has not been robust, the dollar price of oil nevertheless has climbed back to US$ 100 a barrel. Obviously, the question that emerges is whether the secular price of oil has now changed.

It is our contention that the dramatic rise in price followed by an inability of price to equilibrate around the previous historical secular trend is due to the imminence of Peak Oil. Supply manipulation, the chief mechanism that has been used by the oil industry to further their vested interest, is increasingly difficult. The secular price of oil is no longer as easily controlled by the vested interest and must be maintained at a much higher level in order to accommodate nonconventional oil. [1]

1.7. France as a Case Study

After the 1973–1974 oil crisis, and taking into account energy supplies, an oil-importing government's desire to respect the wishes of its oil suppliers seemed more in the national interest than ever before. France was among the first to allow apprehension about oil supply security to influence her relations with Arab states and to back away from close identification with Israel. This was due to the country's higher dependence on oil compared to other European countries: Germany and the UK had coal reserves and oil was 53 and 44 % respectively of their energy mix. For France, this figure was 62 %.

The difference in French reactions to the oil disruptions in 1956 (Suez Crisis) and 1973 illustrates this shift starkly. In 1956, France (and Britain) joined Israel to launch an attack on the Suez Canal, at that time the main passageway for Persian Gulf oil bound for Europe; in 1973 France endorsed the political demands of the Arab states and actively sought 'most friendly' nation status to avoid losing oil supplies. The reasons for France's choice of bilateralism are to be found in its tradition of Gaullist-type policies of political and economic

---

[1] J. Edward Gates • David L. Trauger • Brian Czech: Peak Oil, Economic Growth, and Wildlife Conservation. Springer Science+Business Media New York 2014. P 87: 88

independence. For example, unlike the UK and Germany, the French government had a monopoly on the oil industry. During the 1973 crisis, France was the most fervent opponent of common action within the EEC or the OECD. The French government also signed more bilateral agreements with producers than any other consumer. [1]

As it turned out, however, these actions did not protect France from oil losses, because oil distribution was still under the control of the oil companies, who refused to favor France over their other customers and claimed that their contractual obligations took priority over instructions from their shareholders, i.e. the governments. Therefore, despite being on the Arab "friends" list, France also experienced supply cuts, mostly due to efforts by the companies to allocate oil equally among the final consumers. At the end of November 1973, they notified the French government that they would reduce oil deliveries by 10–15 %. This reduction never materialized, and between December 1973 and March 1974 the availability of petroleum in France was only about 5 % lower than a year earlier.

---

[1]Rossella Bardazzi • Maria Grazia Pazienza Alberto Tonini: European Energy and Climate Security. Springer International Publishing Switzerland 2016. P 24

Nevertheless, the French government's reply was not delayed. If up to 1973 the geographic oil patterns were largely dominated by the major oil companies, after the Arab oil disruption some European governments began to consider ways to gain access to oil supplies directly, skipping the mediation of the oil companies. As soon as the embargo was announced, the French government started negotiations with several Middle Eastern oil producers. For instance, in 1974 the French government pursued special supply arrangements with Saudi Arabia and concluded a contract to buy 200 million barrels over three years. This was an unprecedented incursion into the domain of Aramco, the producing company owned by Exxon, Socal, Mobil and Texaco. France was more ambitious still and sought to make a much larger arrangement with Saudi Arabia, involving 6000 million barrels over twenty years. This deal was discarded because Saudi Arabia would not give France access to oil on the same terms as Aramco enjoyed, and France was unwilling to build an export refinery in Saudi Arabia and agree in advance to import its products.

Besides Saudi Arabia, in 1974 France signed agreements with Iraq, Algeria, and Iran. These deals guaranteed the much-needed oil, but they had no effects in terms of lowering the oil price as most of the contracts were signed at very high prices. While they brought a higher level of security to France, they did not alleviate the most nefarious consequence of the 1973 oil crisis—high prices. [1]

Successive French governments increasingly tailored their foreign policies in the light of the problem of energy security and its economic effects. After this setback, French bilateral agreements with Opec countries usually involved industrial development projects, credits and cultural exchanges, and left oil trade to the established companies. Closer relations with oil exporters were desirable for several reasons. Increased trade would obviously ease French payment problems and might give the oil producers a greater awareness of, and stake in, the importer's welfare.

In effect, this could be a kind of economic deterrence against oil disruptions: in general terms, it was intended to make the oil countries more sensitive to economic changes in their customer. It is doubtful, however, whether the increase in import purchases by the Arab countries created significant economic vulnerability to disruptions in those imports. Many of the industrial goods imported by Opec

---

[1] Rossella Bardazzi • Maria Grazia Pazienza Alberto Tonini: European Energy and Climate Security. Springer International Publishing Switzerland 2016. P 24: 25

states were components of construction projects that would take years to complete. Thus, a trade counter-embargo by France was unlikely to have as dramatic and sudden effect on Saudi Arabia or other Opec members as an oil supply loss had on Western European countries. Moreover, increased exports to Arab states made a rupture in relations all the costlier for France, by giving the oil producers one more option for influencing the oil importer: the threat of suspending purchases of its exports.

Although such a threat was never made, the possibility had to be included in assessing the vulnerability of an oil-importing nation such as France. As with oil supply curtailments, the general trade 'lever' in the hands of Saudi Arabia was the most powerful because it had the most revenue to dispose of. [1]

The French government continued to call for cooperation between oil-producing and consuming countries in order to seek agreement over supply and demand patterns, investment, and other forms of long-term cooperation. While this led to exploratory contacts between representatives of the EEC and OPEC, it did not precipitate dramatic new initiatives.

---

[1]Rossella Bardazzi • Maria Grazia Pazienza Alberto Tonini: European Energy and Climate Security. Springer International Publishing Switzerland 2016. P 25

The French continued to call for dialogue in other forums and sought to promote a "trilogue", grouping Western Europe, Africa and the Arab world, based in part on references to France's historical Mediterranean vocation. Conspicuously absent from this format were both an Atlantic perspective and any role for North America, Eastern Europe, or the Soviet Union. These over-arching diplomatic gestures were also accompanied by tangible individual policies and actions. Among these, arms sales played a particularly important role as a means both of recycling Arab petrodollars to France and of courting certain regimes. For example, during mid-1979 France carried out negotiations with Iraq for arms sales with a potential value of $1.5 billion and made commitments to deliver Mirage F-1 fighter-bombers, missile-launching patrol boats and another advanced weapons system. France also began delivery to Libya of ten missile-launching patrol boats, equipped with surface-to-surface "Otomat" missiles with a range of 160 km—rather more than might be required for a mere coastal defense capability. [1]

---

[1] Rossella Bardazzi • Maria Grazia Pazienza Alberto Tonini: European Energy and Climate Security. Springer International Publishing Switzerland 2016. P 26: 27

2. Worldwide Subsidies to Fossil Energy

Another feature of petroleum and natural gas sales, which makes it difficult to assess the true value of trade in those commodities, is the issue of subsidies.

Many energy-rich countries subsidize oil and natural gas on their domestic markets. Th at is largely because energy exporters tend to have nationalized energy resources and, therefore, as property of the state citizens in those countries often feel they are entitled to the energy themselves. All of OPEC's members have nationalized their energy resources, as have other exporters such as Mexico and Norway. Th e price charged for energy varies between different countries. Venezuela is noted as having the world's cheapest oil at around five cents a liter (19 cents for a gallon) of gasoline, while in Iran it stands at 11 cents for a liter (less than 50 cents a gallon), in Saudi Arabia it is 12 cents per liter (78 cents per gallon), in Kuwait 21 cents per liter (88 cents a gallon), and in Qatar 22 cents per liter (92 cents a gallon).

Subsidized energy prices are not only applied in energy-exporting countries. Importers such as India and China have also subsidized energy costs.

The reasons behind the seemingly illogical policy in energy-importing states are an attempt to help the poor cope with the costs of energy. In India, kerosene is often used by the poorest sectors in cooking, and removing subsidies is seen as hurting that sector. China has been attempting to remove subsidies, and with the drop-in price for oil and natural gas subsidies have slowly been reduced, although the cost of that energy has not dropped because it had been below market rates.

While subsidized, or underpriced, energy costs are generally popular with the citizens of states that provide that energy, there are many who criticize that practice. Th e main condemnations are that subsidies deprive governments of potential revenue and discourage energy conservation. In Iraq and other Persian Gulf states, air conditioners blow full blast in every room of homes even if no one is at home. In Russia, natural gas is used in heating apartment buildings, but often there is no thermostat to regulate the gas so it is simply on or off. When it is off, apartments are as cold as freezers, but when it is on they become sweltering saunas. To remedy the problem and regulate the temperature, Muscovites turn on the gas and then open the windows to cool the apartments. While that works well in getting the temperature to a comfortable level, it represents an enormous waste of energy.

The problem for countries with subsidized or underpriced energy is that once that benefit has been introduced, it is often difficult to roll back. Nigeria experienced protests when former President Goodluck Jonathan attempted to raise the price of oil, so that he backed down from his original plans and implemented only marginal increases in January 2012. In Venezuela, President Nicolas Maduro first proposed raising the price of gasoline in December 2013 and has repeatedly stated the underpriced commodity was costing the country some $12.5 billion a year, but to date he has been unable to enforce any price increase for fear of protests. Th e issue was so sensitive in the country that not even the popular late President Hugo Chavez dared propose such a measure, and the last time an announcement was made in favor of raising oil prices in 1989, by President Carlos Andres Perez, protests erupted in which around 300 people were killed.

The problem of cheap domestic energy has been felt acutely by the Middle East and North African (MENA) countries. Demand for natural gas in MENA grew almost 90% between 2000 and 2010 leading some of those countries to become net importers of natural gas even though the region holds half of the world's proven gas reserves. The cheap price of energy, especially natural gas, led Kuwait to begin importing LNG in 2009. As demand for natural gas has been growing within the MENA region, governments have announced plans to tackle the problem of underpriced domestic supplies, but to date only Iran appears to have made any progress since it began a five-year program to remove subsidies in December 2010.

Iran had a unique set of incentives to reduce energy subsidies. It was under economic sanctions by many members of the international community over its alleged nuclear weapons program which substantially curbed foreign investment in the country. In addition, it offered the highest energy subsidies of all MENA states at some $60–70 billion per year. Its subsidies had made it the world's second largest importer of gasoline in 2005 as it did not have the refining capacity to supply domestic demand. Th at demand was high not only because of domestic consumption but people found that filling up gasoline tanks and selling them in neighboring Turkey for profit provided additional income so they were selling the country's cheap energy outside of Iran. The cheap energy also made Iran the world's third largest consumer of natural gas after the USA and Russia. President Mahmoud Ahmadinejad instituted a program in 2010 raising the price of oil over five years, and natural gas over five to ten years.

Opponents of the removal of energy subsidies have argued that cheap energy helps domestic industries develop and makes them more competitive in the global market. Since energy-exporting states sometimes have an unhealthy dependence on energy revenues, diversifying their economies by developing other sectors is seen as a highly desirable development, and any government plans that could undermine such eff orts are seen as detrimental to the state's interest. Nonetheless, many countries which subsidize or underprice their energy can ill-afford such policies. In Egypt between 2010 and 2011, the government spent $16 billion on energy subsidies, which was more than the $4 billion spent on health in that period, or the $9 billion spent on education. Th e costs of subsidizing and underpricing energy are seen as unsustainable in the long term in most countries engaged in such practices but raising prices has not proved easy and is unlikely to happen quickly. [1]

The widespread use and the scale of energy subsidies would suggest that policymakers are convinced that such subsidies can play an important role in achieving their

---

[1] Thijs Van de Graaf • Benjamin K. Sovacool Arunabha Ghosh • Florian Kern • Michael T. Klare: The Palgrave Handbook of the International Political Economy of Energy. 2016. P 241: 243

policy objectives. But what are the factors underlying the

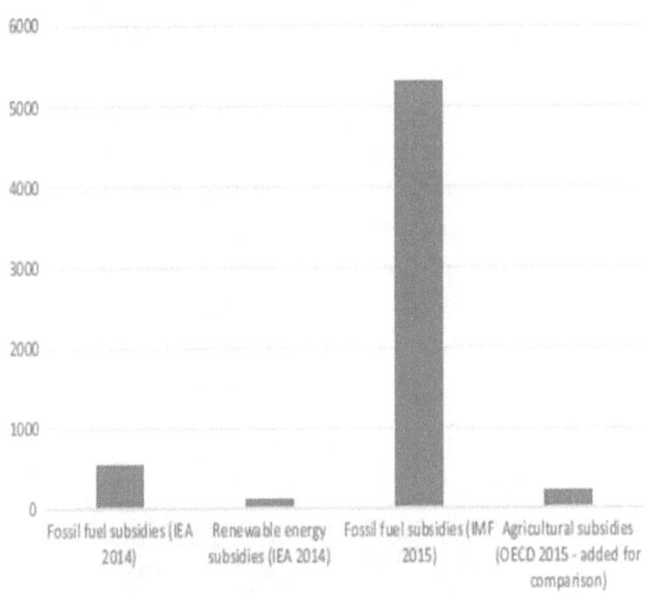

ig. 11.1   Energy subsidy estimates (billion US$)

received scant attention in the literature.

Oosterhuis and Umpfenbach (2014) distinguish four broad types of rationales underpinning energy subsidies. The first three types of explanations are functional: subsidies can help achieve economic, social, and/or environmental objectives. From an economic perspective, subsidies can help reduce dependence on energy imports, or help countries achieve first-mover advantage with respect to the development—and possible export—of new and emerging energy technologies. This has, for instance, been an important rationale for renewable energy support in countries such as the USA and China. Social objectives served by subsidies can include the provision of energy at affordable prices (a major concern particularly in developing countries) but may also relate to the creation or protection of local and national industries and jobs (e.g. the protection of coal miners in Germany).

Energy subsidies, particularly for renewable energy, may further be motivated by the pursuit of environmental objectives, such as climate change mitigation and improving air quality.

The final explanation offered by Oosterhuis and Umpfenbach (2014) is concerned with the political economy of energy subsidies. Energy subsidies can be seen as a rent provided by the politicians to secure the support of interest groups (e.g. energy producers or consumers). Referring to the example of how biofuel subsidies in the USA were adopted and maintained, Victor (2009) suggests that when energy producers are concentrated and well organized, and the costs are distributed across the general population, there will be a strong 'demand' for subsidies. He adds, however, that the 'supply' side of subsidies is at least as important. Subsidies appeal to governments not only because they can help garner political support but also because they are a relatively straightforward tool to achieve such objectives, for instance, compared to cash transfer schemes. Th is 'supply-side' explanation goes some way in explaining why certain autocratic governments (e.g. in the Middle East) hand out sizable fossil fuel consumer subsidies.

However, this explanation is still partial at best, as it is focused primarily at energy producers and exporters. Complementary explanations have been put forward. Cheon et al. (2015), for example, analyze the role of national oil companies in countries providing petroleum subsidies. They suggest that such companies allow governments to respond to oil price fluctuations through subsidies and that in countries such as Iran, Argentina, and India, national oil companies allow governments to hide the fiscal burden of subsidies. Using the example of Indonesia, Lockwood suggests that energy subsidies are particularly prevalent in countries with weak central control, meaning that 'power is too decentralized to coordinate corruption.

Studies on the political economy of renewable energy support are also scarce. Szarka (2010) examines the emergence of policies in support of wind power in the European Union (EU), concluding that it is insufficient to focus on so-termed advocacy coalitions, and arguing that the interests of industries (both incumbents and newcomers) as well as the public interest should be taken into account in the analysis.

Ultimately, it is likely that in any given context, multiple rationales are simultaneously at play, and explanations will need to account for specificities of the countries or regions adopting and maintaining the energy subsidies.

Studying the rationales will remain of high importance, as they shed light not only on why subsidies were adopted in the first place but also on why it can be challenging to reform them. [1]

Energy subsidies may thus be adopted to meet a range of goals. Yet it remains unclear to which extent subsidies actually achieve those aims. Moreover, subsidies may lead to other (unintended) adverse effects.

[1] Thijs Van de Graaf • Benjamin K. Sovacool Arunabha Ghosh • Florian Kern • Michael T. Klare: The Palgrave Handbook of the International Political Economy of Energy. 2016. P 272: 274

In terms of economic effects, a first-order impact of subsidies is the burden they pose on the public purse. With respect to fossil fuel subsidies, the IMF suggests that eliminating post-tax subsidies could free up $2.9 trillion in government revenues. Again, there is variation between countries. For instance, fuel subsidies took up 13.7% of the government budget in India in the 2012–2013 fi scal year (IISD 2014); this number is higher in some countries in the Middle East and North Africa region, where subsidies have taken up to 35% of the government budget. Th is not only matters from the perspective of government revenues; in developing countries, it also matters as the money could have been spent on other issues for which there is social demand, such as health, education, or public infrastructure.

Th is ties in to the social impacts of fossil fuel subsidies. While expanding energy access for the poor may be a rationale for fuel subsidies, such subsidies tend to be highly regressive, meaning that they mainly benefit the richer part of the population. For instance, in India, $8 billion of fuel subsidies for liquefied petroleum gas largely failed to reach the rural poor. Based on a review of fuel subsidies in 20 developing countries, Arze del Granado and Coady (2012, p. 2241) conclude that 'the richest 20% of households capture on average six times more in fuel subsidies than the poorest 20%'.

For gasoline, the effects are strongest, with 'over 97 out of every 100 dollars of gasoline subsidy [leaking] to the top four quintiles. One of the underlying reasons is that the wealthy generally consume more energy; however, politically informed handouts may also play a part.

In terms of environmental impacts, Stefanski (2014) suggests that 36% of global carbon emissions between 1980 and 2010 were driven by fossil fuel subsidies.

Conversely, there are various estimates of the climate change mitigation benefits of fossil fuel subsidy removal. Burniaux and Chateau (2014) estimate that if the 37 countries covered by IEA analyses remove consumer subsidies between 2013 and 2020, this would lead to a reduction of global greenhouse gas emissions by 8%. Th e IMF—whose definition, it should be remembered, is wider—estimates that eliminating post-tax subsidies could result in carbon dioxide emission reductions of over 20%. Country specific analyses have also emerged. For example, Lin and Ouyang (2014) estimate that the removal of consumer subsidies in China in 2006–2010 led to emissions savings of 3.72% of total emissions during that period. Th ere are also indirect impacts of fossil fuel subsidies (and their reform) on emissions: such subsidies lower the relative costs of fossil fuels vis-à-vis renewable energy technologies, strengthen the power of fossil fuel industries as incumbents, and distort investment decisions against renewable energy. Vice versa, however, if the savings of fossil fuel subsidy reform are invested in renewables or energy efficiency, this may bring about additional mitigation benefits.

The effects of renewable energy subsidies are difficult to estimate, as much will depend on the interaction with policies to promote renewable energy and other climate policies, notably carbon pricing. Kalkuhl et al. (2013) suggest that, on their own, renewable energy subsidies constitute an expensive way of reducing emissions. Nevertheless, such subsidies have helped kick-start local and national renewable energy industries—notably wind—in some countries, such as Denmark and Germany, and may help other countries, such as China, achieve a range of economic, social, and environmental goals. However, whether renewable energy subsidies are able to simultaneously achieve various goals remains unclear: in India, support for wind and solar photovoltaic helped to achieve energy security and environmental goals but was less successful in creating new jobs and establishing an internationally competitive industry (Ganesan et al. 2014). Moreover, not all renewable energy subsidies will have positive environmental impacts: subsidies for some types of renewable energy—for example, bioenergy and (large) hydro—may also lead to adverse environmental impacts. [1]

Energy subsidies are measures and practices that keep energy prices for energy producers and end users below marginal costs of clean energy production or consumption. Producer subsidies often arise when state-owned energy enterprises, power utility for example, are inefficient and have high costs of production because of non-payment or low payment of bills from government agencies and power distribution losses. The International Monetary Fund stated that worldwide post-tax subsidies, which are the sum of pre-tax and tax subsidies, amounted to US$1.9 trillion or 2.7 % of the total GDP of the world in 2012. Subsidies to fossil energy encourage excessive fossil energy production and consumption, which accelerates the depletion of natural resources. They also reduce the incentive for investment in energy efficiency. If the amount of US$1.9 trillion capital was invested annually in energy efficiency, the world could have closed the energy efficiency investment gap. [2]

---

[1]Thijs Van de Graaf • Benjamin K. Sovacool Arunabha Ghosh • Florian Kern • Michael T. Klare: The Palgrave Handbook of the International Political Economy of Energy. 2016. P 274: 276

[2]Ming Yang • Xin Yu: Energy Efficiency Benefits for Environment and Society. Springer-Verlag London 2015. P

The group of 20 advanced and emerging market economies (G20) initially called for phasing out inefficient fossil fuel subsidies in all countries in 2009 and reaffirmed this again in 2012. Despite the global policy and strategy, many countries have had difficulty phasing out subsidies. When subsidy reform takes place, prices increase which often leads to widespread public complaints and protests. Governments are also often concerned that higher energy prices will contribute to a higher rate of inflation and adversely affect their competitiveness. Subsidy reform can also be complex when the purpose is to reduce inefficiencies and production costs. For example, in a public-owned power sector, utilities are used to government regulatory policy that guarantees their minimum return in operation. Reforming subsidy will force these power utilities to adapt new and changing electricity market, which may cause loss of revenue and loss of jobs to the utility companies. While there is no single recipe for successful subsidy reform, the IMF (2013) suggests the following to overcome the energy subsidy barrier: [1]

---

[1] Ming Yang • Xin Yu: Energy Efficiency Benefits for Environment and Society. Springer-Verlag London 2015. P 35

1. a comprehensive energy sector reform plan with clear long-term objectives with an analysis of the impact of reforms;

2. transparent and extensive communication and consultation with stakeholders, including information on the size of subsidies and how they affect the government's budget;

3. price increases that are phased in over time;

4. improving the efficiency in state-owned enterprises to reduce producer subsidies;

5. measures to protect the poor through targeted cash or near-cash transfers or, if this option is not feasible, a focus on existing targeted programs that can be expanded quickly; and

6. institutional reforms that depoliticize energy pricing, such as the introduction of automatic pricing mechanisms.

2.1. Subsidized prices or fiscal revenues?

In most developing countries, domestic energy prices are regulated and the resulting low prices available make these projects relatively unattractive to producers.

In many countries, the inability of local consumers to pay anything like the international market prices for gas has traditionally meant that developing gas for domestic use has been considered uneconomic by investors, who are mostly interested in exporting gas to the more lucrative markets in North America, Europe, Japan and Korea.

The increase in energy prices between 2002 and mid 2008 has slowly been reflected in increasing domestic prices in developing countries, and interest in local projects is growing among producers, not least because of the surge in costs associated with exporting gas, whether by long-distance pipeline or LNG.

With a strong political desire in most countries to expand local gas utilization, the more the economic differential between domestic and export sales is reduced, the more attractive local projects will become. However, the transition from the current price structure in most developing countries to one comparable to that prevailing in the main consumer countries will take time.

In the meantime, to encourage development of gas supplies for domestic utilization, governments are beginning to require gas producers pursuing export projects to include a component of domestic gas utilization. For example, a new LNG project may require producers to also provide feedstock to a local power plant, as part of the overall development. Without the domestic commitment, the export project will not be approved. Thus, producers are obliged to supply the local market, although they will tend to keep their involvement in supplying gas to buyers as far upstream as possible.

Where prices are below the costs of production, the only way investors can be persuaded to develop the gas is if the government provides a subsidy – either explicitly or implicitly through some form of consolidation with oil production.

Nigeria, for example, got around a similar economic impasse by allowing oil producers to consolidate the capital costs of gas utilization projects to be recovered from oil revenues, thus attracting 85 per cent tax relief, while allowing any operating profits to be taxed under standard corporate tax rules, at a 30 per cent rate. Under certain circumstances, the tax generated from the production would be less than the tax relief allowed up front – an implicit subsidy for the oil producers.

Investors claim that without this fiscal incentive, local gas prices – including the feed gas price the Nigerian LNG ('NLNG') project pays – are not high enough to enable economic development of the reserves. There has been much debate over the fiscal rules for gas projects in Nigeria in the past few years, but a new fiscal regime has yet to emerge (3Q 2008).

Where there is a significant divergence between domestic and export prices for gas, governments can either incentivize domestic projects through lower taxation or explicit subsidies to producers. Alternatively, they can reduce the economic attractiveness of export projects by levying an export duty on production. This can reduce the netback price to equate to the price available in the domestic market.

There are a number of countries which impose such duties on oil exports, but only a small number apply export duties to gas, notably Argentina and Russia. [1]

---

[1] Philip Daniel, Michael Keen and Charles McPherson: The Taxation of Petroleum and Minerals. international Monetary Fund. 2010. P 181: 182

2.2. Gross royalty

Royalty can be a per-unit tax, which is a uniform fixed charge levied on a specified level of volume of production or an ad-valorem tax, which is a fixed charge levied on the value of the output (gross revenues). Royalty rates for oil are generally set in a range from 5 per cent to 25 per cent but most are nearer 10 per cent to 15 per cent of production. Natural gas is often assigned a lower rate than oil.

Royalty holds its attractions to host governments. Royalty is relatively simple to administer, predictable and provides an early revenue stream as soon as production starts. The optics of early revenues for the government minimizes the political risk of further intervention.

But as the royalty is not profit related, it may deter marginal projects that are profitable on a pre-tax basis from proceeding. The regressive nature of royalty – the lower is project profitability, the higher are royalty payments relative to profits – can cause operating income to become negative even when gross revenues exceed extraction costs, and consequently can lead to a premature abandonment of the field. Royalty directly reduces the quantities of reported production and booked reserves for companies (which analysts and media commentators take interest in as one of the performance indicators for IOCs in stock markets, although booked reserves are not directly linked to profitability), unlike other tax elements. For instance, a royalty of 15 per cent results in only 85 per cent of the reserves being booked under a Tax and Royalty regime.

In mature high cost basins such as the UK and Norway, royalty has been Progressively eliminated. Some nations are more attached to a strong royalty tradition, particularly the US, where royalty rates in the US GoM have increased from 12.5 per cent to 16.66 per cent. Other countries have introduced a profit element in royalties by having them depend on the level of production (like China) or in some cases oil price. This is known as a sliding scale royalty, where the royalty rate is low when production or oil price is low and vice versa, thereby decreasing the possibility of negative cash flows when production or oil prices are low.

Royalty is normally allowable as a deduction against other taxes, such as field-based taxes (like the PRT in the UK) and income taxes. [1]

---

[1] Philip Daniel, Michael Keen and Charles McPherson: The Taxation of Petroleum and Minerals. international Monetary Fund. 2010. P 95: 96

2.3. Monopoly and Competition in the Oil Industry

The existence of the dominant but erroneous concept of monopoly is common to all the prevailing views on the oil crisis. Without exception, all the existing theories, either implicitly or explicitly, tend to agree that the price of oil is directly determined by the OPEC cartel, or through the monopoly of oil firms, or both. For instance, the dependency theory of the oil crisis implies that oil prices prior to the events of the early 1970s were determined by the oil companies, but after the "OPEC offensive," which was a move against unequal exchange at the international level, they were set by the oil-exporting countries.

The conspiracy theory argues that the increase in the price of oil was primarily initiated by the US government in conjunction with the major oil firms and the concerted effort of OPEC. The conventional theory of the oil crisis contends that controls of the production, distribution, and marketing operations do not allow the laws of supply and demand to operate properly. Therefore, competition is imperfect (Salant 1982, Robinson 1969, among others) for the scholars who invest their model on the illusory and idealized notion of "pure competition" to present a realistic picture, having little grasp of the fact that the reality is what there is—it is neither perfect nor imperfect. The common denominator of all these views is the quantitative theory of competition and monopoly. The notion of monopoly is perceived to be dependent upon the number of firms within the industry. Accordingly, if the number of firms operating in an industry is small, it is called a "monopoly" or an "oligopoly." On the other hand, if the numbers of firms in an industry are many, it is believed that competition prevails.

In contrast with the above views, since competition and centralization of capital (i.e., monopoly) are not mutually exclusive in the process of the production of value, one cannot talk about monopoly without competition. The formation of value in an industry in general, and in the oil industry in particular, necessarily emerges through competition. In the oil industry, just like in any other industry, competition among different production units, with different individual values, leads to the formation of social value for the entire industry.

In addition, production of oil is intertwined with the formation of rent, which in turn develops through competition (Fine 1983, Bina 1985). Thus, competition as an inner nature of capital will always be present in the process of accumulation and value formation.

Accordingly, the competitive struggle among capitals leads to concentration, centralization, and the further integration of capital in the accumulation process; this competition leads to integration and further integration leads to further competition. As a result, it is hardly surprising that the existing theories all failed to recognize the true nature of the oil crisis of 1973–74, and the significance of post crisis developments. [1]

---

[1] Cyrus Bina: A Prelude to the Foundation of Political Economy. PALGRAVE MACMILLAN. 2013. P 41:42

3. Natural Gas as a Game-Changer

The share of natural gas among sources of primary energy is rising faster than that of oil and coal. At the same time, the gas industry is undergoing immense changes as new technologies, demand and supply patterns create new market forces.

In 2011, after the Fukushima nuclear accident, the International Energy Agency heralded the arrival of a "golden age" of gas in the period until 2035 due to enormous economic growth in China combined with significant gas consumption, a low share of nuclear energy in the generation of electricity, an increase in the use of gas in the transportation sector, and a boom in unconventional gas production and subsequently lower prices. Electricity from renewable resources still requires natural gas as a back-up energy source because an uninterrupted supply of renewable energy is not available – at least until technology enabling the high-efficiency storage of electricity is discovered and commercialized.

Unconventional gas is becoming a real game changer in the US gas market. The widespread adoption of techniques such as hydraulic fracturing and horizontal drilling, have made those reserves much more accessible, and, in the case of natural gas, has resulted in a glut that has sent prices plunging. The "shale gale" sweeping across North America the past few years has more than doubled the size of discovered natural gas resources in North America – enough to satisfy more than 100 years of consumption at current rates, according to a major new analysis of the leading unconventional gas plays in North America by IHS Cambridge Energy Research Associates.

In 2010, 12 billion cubic meters (bcm) of LNG was imported into the US. Before this unconventional gas revolution, this number was expected to reach 140 bcm by 2020. Now, the US is set to become a major natural gas exporter, transforming the global gas market. The price of gas sold by Henry Hub in the U.S. dropped in 2012 to a level of $2 per million metric British thermal unit (MMBtu), its lowest level in the past decade, while the European average spot price and oil-indexed price have fluctuated between $8 and $10, and the Japanese averaged around $17.

If the Henry Hub price remains near $3, LNG exports of domestic production look very competitive at anticipated prices in Europe. If the Henry Hub price is raised and a higher price event or set of events happens, such that a $10 spike is tenable, then exports look out of the question. A future price level that could accommodate a $10 price spike also could be more attractive to LNG imports.

The US success story has inspired many other countries, including Argentina, China, Poland, South Africa and the UK, to develop their own reserves. Shale development in China, home to the world's largest shale deposits, has been slower than predicted by the government. China may produce 6.5 bcm of shale gas annually by 2015 and has set a target of 60–100 bcm of production annually by 2020, according to China's National Development and Reform Commission.

However, as yet, no country other than the US has what could be termed a shale gas industry – gas production from tight oil and shale plays is still negligible outside the US. Most production increases will only come after 2020, as countries need time to develop the commercial unconventional gas sector due to various geological, logistical and regulatory challenges. The countries where shale gas is presumed to exist in the EU are Germany, Poland, Sweden, France, Austria, Hungary and the UK. Warsaw is harboring major ambitions to develop shale gas, the switch towards which is like "the twenty-first century's gold rush".

But, shale gas cannot yet be seen as a game changer in Europe as it is in the US, where roughly 50 % of the country's needs are met by developing unconventional gas. To illustrate the possible impact of developing shale gas in Europe, the U.S. Geological Survey pointed out that in an area the size of the Benelux countries, there would have to be up to 6,000 wells, an impact that would probably attract environmental opposition. The reason for such concentration is that unlike natural gas, unconventional gas needs a high density of wells, including horizontal wells.

Another development that has transformed and continues to transform the landscape of the natural gas industry is the advent of Liquefied Natural Gas (LNG). This mode of transport allows gas-exporting countries to ship their gas over long distances and releases them from the traditional dependence issues associated with pipelines. Pipelines are expensive and, once built, tie producers and consumers together indefinitely, while LNG allows both exporting and importing countries to escape this form of captivity. Understandably, this has both commercial as well as geopolitical consequences.

Between now and through 2015, several Southeast Asian countries will emerge as new LNG importers and demand in existing markets will increase steadily. On the supply side, however, only a small number of new projects are coming on line; these are the Pluto LNG project in West Australia, the Angolan LNG project, and the Algerian LNG project. Consequently, the world LNG market will likely tighten up. However, the final impact remains uncertain: the prevailing European economic crisis may keep demand sluggish or prolonged shutdowns of nuclear power plants in Japan may keep demand for LNG high.

In 2011, final investment decisions were made for several LNG plants that will go on stream in the Pacific basin in 2015 or later. These projects, if commissioned without delay, would contribute to stabilize the LNG market in the long-run. In addition, new prospective supply sources are coming up in East African countries like Mozambique. At the same time, LNG exports from North America are emerging rapidly as a next-generation supply source. The Sabine Pass project, which has recently fixed sales agreements for 16 million tons, uses low-cost gas brought about by the shale gas revolution.

Despite the rise of LNG, pipelines are still the backbone of the gas industry.

Transport by pipeline is not as flexible as by LNG tanker, but is often the cheapest method, depending on the geographical location. Coal, oil and gas, particularly natural gas, will continue to play an important role, Abundant, affordable and acceptable – gas is a triple-A source of energy. It is cleaner than coal; gas-fired generation is relatively quick and inexpensive to build; and the shale revolution in North America has raised hopes that gas is abundant in geological formations the world over. [1]

---

[1] Andre' Dorsman • Timur Go"k • Mehmet Baha Karan: Perspectives on Energy Risk. Springer-Verlag Berlin Heidelberg 2014. P 14: 16

4. environmental pollution

Since the late 1970s, the problems of energy safety, environmental pollution, and climate change were becoming increasingly severe. On the one hand, many countries (especially developed countries) have accelerated the development of alternative and renewable energies to counter these problems. On the other hand, despite the influence and constraints of national policy, as well as the cost and technology, the ratio of fossil fuels has continued to remain relatively high, even showing an increasing trend in some countries. Developed countries have many technological advantages over developing countries in renewable energy production, but the ratio of renewable energy, excluding hydropower, has not increased significantly in terms of primary energy production. [1]

From 1970 to 2000, Germany, Italy, Japan, and other countries, which attached great importance to environmental protection or significantly lacked fossil fuels, have paid much attention to renewable electric power generation and its production ratio increased accordingly. In some countries, such as the United States, Canada, UK, and France, the ratio showed no

---

[1] Yi-Ming Wei • Hua Liao: Energy Economics: Energy Efficiency in China. Springer International Publishing Switzerland 2016. P 22

increase and sometimes it even decreased. Since 2000, with the soaring fossil fuel prices and the increasing need for countries to adapt to climate change, renewable energy has gained unprecedented attention from both developed countries, such as the United States, EU, and Japan, and developing countries, such as China, India, and Brazil. [1]

China is also a major producer of carbon dioxide with a rapid growth in emissions. Although there are no specific greenhouse gas reduction obligations at present, the worsening of global climate change issues and the growing emissions of greenhouse gas in China will result in greater efforts to mitigate carbon emissions in the future. Since the Industrial Revolution, the largest amount of the global accumulation of greenhouse gases was discharged by the developed countries and the per capita emissions of China are currently only about 35 % of those in the OECD countries. Even though the cost of reducing greenhouse gas emissions is high, developed countries have already completed the process of industrialization and they have had almost no pressure to reduce their emissions of greenhouse gases during that process. However, China is in the process of industrialization, so it has to not <u>only support its economic</u>

───────────────

[1] Yi-Ming Wei • Hua Liao: Energy Economics: Energy Efficiency in China. Springer International Publishing Switzerland 2016. P 22

development and social progress but also cope with the new challenges posed by global climate change simultaneously. [1]

Because of global climate change and high energy prices, the US government has significantly increased its energy-saving intervention efforts. Congress frequently passes energy-related laws and regulations. According to the National Energy Policy Act passed in 2005, the US will cut taxes ($14.6 billion) for all US energy enterprises within 10 years to encourage these enterprises (including oil, gas, coal, and electric power) to take appropriate measures on energy conversation and environmental protection. The Federal Energy Legislation passed in 2007 drew up more detailed plans for automobile fuel economy standards, equipment energy standards, industrial standards, regional energy savings, and so on. Furthermore, although the US did not sign the Kyoto Protocol, several state governments have proposed specific targets for saving energy and reducing emissions. In 2006, the state of California passed the Global Warming Solutions Act, which was the first cap-scheme bill for greenhouse gases in the country. In 2007, the US Congress passed the United States Climate Security Act to cut greenhouse

---

[1]Yi-Ming Wei • Hua Liao: Energy Economics: Energy Efficiency in China. Springer International Publishing Switzerland 2016. P 48: 49

gas emissions and maintain strong economic growth. So far, these bills have played an important role in various forms and the states have pursued various energy-saving methods. A $168 billion economic stimulus bill was enacted by the US in February 2009. This bill almost included all of the economic aspects and new energy policies, as clean sources of power and energy conservation were the key points of the bill. The new energy policies of this bill were universally recognized by American society. The American Clean Energy and Security Act was designed to reduce greenhouse gas emissions in the US and was narrowly passed by the House of Representatives in July 2009. Title 2 of this Act is about energy efficiency, including some specific items about architectural lighting, the transportation industry, and household energy use. [1]

In terms of government procurement, the EU actively supports "green" procurement activities by the public, claiming that the contracts of green public procurement should include the terms of environmental protection and step-up efforts to reform the energy-saving product technologies and services. Due to the government procurement accounting standard, which is supposed to represent 16 % of GDP, the

---

[1] Yi-Ming Wei • Hua Liao: Energy Economics: Energy Efficiency in China. Springer International Publishing Switzerland 2016. P 278

EU promotes and supports the markets of energy-saving products and services so as to accelerate their distribution and boost the confidence of markets to purchase products that conserve energy. In terms of promoting energy conservation, the EU invested an additional 3.6 million euros to launch its program entitled "EU Sustainable Energy in 2005–2008." At the same time, it also utilized various kinds of public media platforms in the hopes of publicizing and increasing the public's awareness of saving energy. [1]

With the emerging It stands to reason that understanding energy efficiency in the climate policy discourse is associated with finding policy instruments that make use of the same mode of action or that are at least compatible with the main carbon abatement policy instrument, namely, emissions trading.

climate change discourse, increasing energy efficiency and thus reducing energy demand is perceived as one means to achieve carbon emission reductions in a fast and cost-effective manner. Tradable permits, carbon taxes, and carbon offsets are policy instruments that have gained prominence within the climate

---

[1] Yi-Ming Wei • Hua Liao: Energy Economics: Energy Efficiency in China. Springer International Publishing Switzerland 2016. P 285: 286

change discourse and are often referred to as market-based policy instruments. Thus, the three discourses of energy efficiency, formed around the goals of securing energy at affordable prices, maintaining competitiveness and combating climate change imply different problems to be solved. Within each discourse, the ultimate goals translate into more concrete, shorter-term goals such as reducing CO_2 emissions, reducing electricity consumption, reducing gas consumption, reducing the peak load, market penetration of a certain energy-efficiency standards, promoting innovative technology, and so forth. Each perspective offers an understanding of energy efficiency from a slightly different angle, and therefore implies a distinct solution. Protecting the climate and ensuring an affordable supply of energy is, for example, not necessarily related to energy savings but rather to carbon savings through energy efficiency or securing a comfort level in all households. Choosing instruments to foster end-use energy efficiency therefore has to take into account the particular goals that end-use energy efficiency aims to address. And this goal is typically located in one or several discourses of energy efficiency. [1]

---

[1] Dagmar Sibyl Steuwer: Energy Efficiency Governance. Springer Fachmedien Wiesbaden 2013. P 93: 94

Britain recognized the global threat of climate change comparatively early. Two documents influenced the development of the instruments of British climate policy from 1990: The Pearce Report (Pearce, Markandya & Barbier 1989) and the Marshall Report (Marshall 1998). While stemming from the 1970s, the discussion about energy taxes gained prominence through the Pearce Report to the environmental ministry. Well-known as the 'Blueprint for a Green Economy', the report praised the cost-effectiveness of taxes and their ability to internalize external costs as compared with tradition command-and-control regulation. The Marshall Report also concluded that economic instruments would play a major role in climate policy alongside more traditional regulatory approaches. Lord Marshall identified two leading options: emission trading schemes and taxes. In the follow-up, the Conservative government introduced a value added tax (VAT) on domestic fuels (with a tax level from zero to eight per cent) in 1993. The decision encountered serious opposition claiming that the tax would disproportionately burden the fuel poor. As a consequence, a planned further increase of the tax level from eight per cent to 17.5 per cent was abandoned. While the UK is often seen as a front-runner in the use of MBIs, not least because of these two influential reports, an analysis by Jordan et al. (2003) revealed that throughout the 1990s the uptake of these policy instruments was not as advanced as often thought:

Until very recently, there was very little interest in and use of MBIs. The idea that MBIs might one day be designed and adopted at a central government level, jarred with the founding precepts of UK policy, which are pragmatism, legalism, secrecy, decentralism and informality. These institutional barriers could have been overcome if the political pressure to change had been there, but it was not. In the 1990s, the small amount of political and institutional space available was used by the Treasury and the DETR to implement 'implicit' taxes. These had more to do with raising revenues than protecting the environment. [1]

The detrimental effects of the naturally gas hydrate dissociation and the gas recovery from gas hydrates have been debated. As commented by Beauchamp, many researchers believed that, if released in the environment, the methane from hydrates would be a significant hazard to marine ecosystems, coastal populations and infrastructures, or worse, would dangerously contribute to global warming. But evidence indicated that the greatest threat to gas hydrate stability in oceanic settings does not

[1] Dagmar Sibyl Steuwer: Energy Efficiency Governance. Springer Fachmedien Wiesbaden 2013. P 238

come from minor environmental fluctuations, but rather from the buildup of free gas beneath the gas hydrate stability zone, which leads to over pressurizing and catastrophic release of gas through pockmarks expulsion,

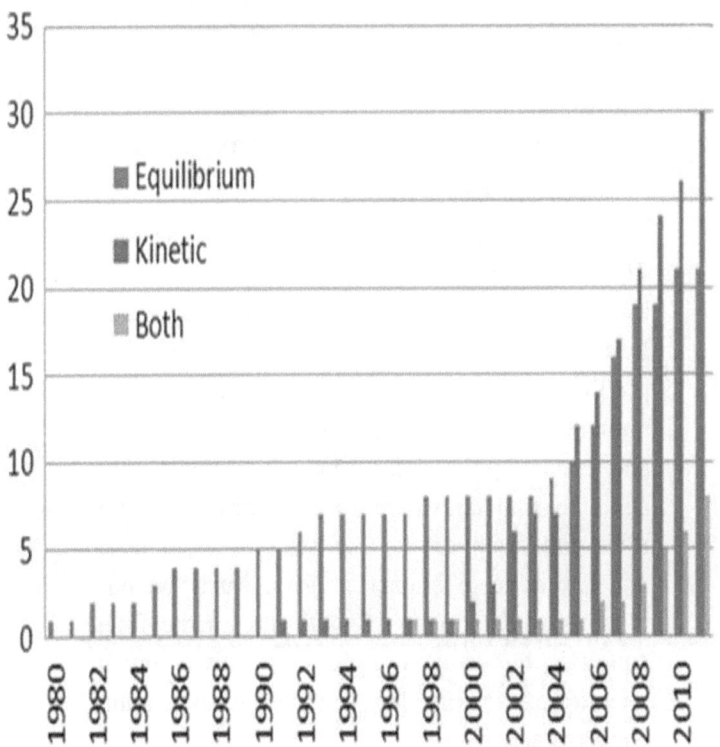

volcanoes, or surface seepage. A truth conflicting with the assumed threats of released gas during gas recovery processes is that methane has to bypass normal fermentation processes to be a warming agent and thus needs to be released very quickly and massively. However, that type of releasing process is impossible within a conventional recovery process. Therefore, while more and more research has been launched due to the possible detrimental effects of gas hydrate dissociation, attention may also be needed to identify solid evidence to support the original judgment. [1]

4.1. Carbon Fuels and Climate: Facts and Uncertainties

Ironically, the same carbon-bearing fuels that drove technological progress and brought us the prosperity and high standard of living are now being blamed for a host of problems and miseries of the present-day life: unbreathable air and premature deaths, oil spills and catastrophic explosions, unbearably hot summers and unusually strong hurricanes, acid rains and disappearance of bio species, and so on. The adverse impact of fossil fuels on our planet's environment, climate and, in the final analysis, our way of life has drawn much attention during the last decades. Among main concerns are:

• Tens of billion tons of anthropogenic CO_2 and other GHG emissions that are released straight

[1] Congrui Jin • Gianluca Cusatis: New Frontiers in Oil and Gas Exploration. Springer International Publishing Switzerland 2016. P 99: 100

to the atmosphere, where they will stay for hundreds of years and impact our planet's ecosystems

• Release into the atmosphere of significant amounts of neurotoxic metals— mercury (Hg) and arsenic (As) by coal-fired power plants

• Emission of sulfur and nitrogen oxides and particulate matter from burning low-quality coals and petroleum products

• Millions of gallons of oil spilled into the environment (During the accident at The Deepwater Horizon rig 185 million gallons of oil was released into the Gulf of Mexico in 2010, the total ecological impact of which we may never know.)

• Practicing controversial mining techniques (e.g., coal industry is now practicing a "mountaintop removal" method of extraction in many coal deposit sites, where the top of a mountain is blasted off)

• The full extent of the ecological impact of hydraulic fracturing technology that extracts NG and oil from shale beds is still unclear.

Some disquieting signs of the adverse impact of the increased usage of fossil fuels on our planet's ecosystems and climate have already started manifesting themselves in the form of retreating glaciers, rising sea levels, shifting rainfall patterns, stronger and more frequent hurricanes, increasing floods, etc. In the years between 1951 and 1980, extremely hot temperatures covered less than 0.2 % of the planet; now this expanded to about 10 % of the land area. The 2003 heat wave in Europe, 2010 heat wave in Russia, 2011 drought in Texas, 2012 wildfires across Australia, 2012 superstorm Sandy in the USA: too many extreme weather events in relatively short time period to consider them a natural weather variation.

In its 2013 Assessment Report, IPCC states that *"Warming of the climate system is unequivocal, and since the 1950s, many of the observed changes are unprecedented over decades to millennia."*. According to the report, human fingerprints have been detected in

- Warming of the atmosphere and the ocean

- Changes in global water cycle

- Reductions in snow and ice

- Global mean sea level rise

- Changes in some climate extremes

The globally averaged combined land and ocean surface temperature increased by 0.85 °C (the range of 0.65–1.06 °C). The report provides data showing that there is 90 % certainty that 1981–2010 was the warmest span in the last eight centuries and 66 % chance that it was the warmest 30-year period in the last 1,400 years (although last 15 years have not warmed as quickly).

The authors of a recent study reported in the *Science* magazine reconstructed regional and global temperature anomalies for the past 11,300 years (to distinguish anthropogenic influences on climate from natural variability) (this rebuts the arguments of critics of climate change research, who try to make a case that all the current studies cover short periods of time, typically, 1,500–2,000 years, and they do not take into account warming the Earth experienced many thousands of years ago due to natural causes.). The study showed that the 1900–1909 decade was colder than 95 % of the last 11,300 years, whereas the decade of 2000–2009 was hotter than 75 % of the last 11,300 years. Thus, the Earth's climate was propelled from one of its coldest decades since the last ice age to one of its hottest—in just one century: a very short period of time for such a spike.

Variations due to the Earth's tilt and orbit and other natural factors cannot explain this sudden anomalous increase in global temperature, which "incidentally" coincided with the surge in the consumption of fossil fuels; just in contrary, based on the historical trends related to the Earth's tilt and position relative to the sun, our planet is supposed to be cooling. The majority of climate scientists hold that if carbon emissions continue to rise, as currently projected, by 2100, global temperatures will rise well above anything seen in the last eleven millennia. If that scenario will prove true, this would bring a misery to hundreds of millions of people around the world over the span of several generations. Does all this imply that we will be paying an increasingly heavy environmental toll for the economic prosperity brought about by fossil fuels?

Despite an access to capable scientific instrumentation and extremely sophisticated computer models, climate scientists are far from understanding all the observations and sometimes unexpected trends; for example, they are struggling to explain a slowdown in climate warming in the last decade. Predominantly focused on century-long climate trends, most climate models failed to predict the slowdown trend in the average temperature rise starting at the turn of the current century and millennium (i.e., around 2000). This exposed some gaps in the understanding of many climatic phenomena and, as could be expected, provided more ammunition to those who question the link between the growth in GHG emissions and rise in planet's mean temperature and climate change. Although many scientists expect a revival of the warming trend in the coming years, they have hard time to determine whether the current break will be a brief or more lasting phenomenon.

According to IPCC, the temperature records since 1850 indicate fluctuations of 10–15 years in duration, but the overall warming trend is unmistakable. Among explanations of the warming slowdown are theories that the deep oceans have taken up more heat leading to cooler surface than expected, or that industrial pollution produced by booming Asian economies is blocking the sun, or that GHG trap less heat that previously thought, or it could be a result of an observed decline in heat-trapping water vapor in the atmosphere at high altitude, or a combination of different factors and unknown or poorly understood natural variations. Regardless of the scientific basis behind the current counterintuitive observations, these uncertainties do not reinforce trust in climate science among general population, although many appreciate the complexity of the climate system.

There is also a lack of agreement among the climate scientists with regard to long-term impact of past CO2 emissions on present and future global mean temperatures. One school of thought holds that even if humankind moves quickly and starts cutting CO2 emissions at unprecedented rates, global temperatures would still continue to rise for many years due to two types of inertia:

• Thermal inertia of the oceans (the estimated value of the temperature rise is about 0.6 °C, in addition to 0.76 °C rise that has already occurred

• Institutional or infrastructural inertia (fossil fuel infrastructure that currently powers 80 % of the world economy represents an extremely large investment; it will ensure that emissions will continue for decades to come Some climate experts go even further and claim that even if the atmospheric CO2 concentrations would remain fixed at the current level, there still be additional future warming due to past emissions; this implies that the increase in the Earth's global temperature is inevitable regardless of the scope of carbon emission reduction.

For example, IPCC in its Fourth Assessment Report (2007) states that "*Adaptation will be necessary to address impacts resulting from the warming which is already* unavoidable due to past emissions. Past emissions are estimated to involve some unavoidable warming (about a further 0.6 °C by the end of the century relative to 1980-1999) even if atmospheric greenhouse gas concentrations remain at 2000 levels". In its 2013 Assessment Report, IPCC held to the same viewpoint "Surface temperatures will remain approximately constant at elevated levels for many centuries after a complete cessation of net anthropogenic CO_2 emissions. Due to the long-time scales of heat transfer from the ocean surface to depth, ocean warming will continue for centuries".

In an article in Science magazine, Matthews and Solomon debate this viewpoint. According to the authors, because of the equal and opposing effects of physical climate inertia and carbon cycle inertia, there is practically no delayed warming due to the past CO_2 emissions. This implies that if CO_2 emissions were to cease immediately, global average temperatures would not increase and remain nearly constant for many centuries. In other words, any further increase in CO_2-induced warming would entirely result from the current CO_2 emissions, and warming at the end of this century will be caused by the cumulative CO2 emissions humankind produces between now and then. But the main (optimistic) conclusion of this study is that future warming is not unavoidable: any tangible reductions in man-made CO2 emissions would lead to an immediate drop in the rate of global climate change. All these conflicting views on the future climate impact of anthropogenic CO2 show that despite advances in computer modeling and accumulated knowledge in the field, climate science is far from understanding of all the climate-related phenomena that could affect humans in not so distant future.

Public opinion on the climate change issue and the human link is as conflicting as some theories and concepts in climate change science. Although the world has seen a steady trend of increasingly hot years, public's belief in climate change has remained relatively stagnant over the past decade. Ironically, recent polls show that people are more likely to believe in climate change during hot years, when they are starting to see global warming as an important issue. According to one survey study, Americans' opinions on climate change literally "blow with the wind"—with more concern shown in the years that are much warmer or much colder than normal.

The study also shows that most Americans (and, probably, the majority of the world's population) aren't steadfast in their opinions on climate change, whether they are believers or skeptics; their opinion is malleable depending on the weather.

A report published by the UK Energy Research Centre shows that 19 % of people do not believe climate change is real—up from just 4 % in 2005—while 9 % did not know. Climate change skeptics do not constitute a homogeneous crowd; among them, it is easy to distinguish three main types:

• "Die-hard" deniers who refute the very possibility of global warming; they claim the data presented by IPCC and other scientific bodies are misleading, their models cannot be trusted, "the Earth is actually cooling not warming," "weather is not climate," etc.

• Skeptics admitting that the climate change may be real, but the available data do not provide a solid proof that human activities are to blame; the real cause of the change is still unknown.

• Skeptics believing that climate change is solely due to natural cycles and variations, and humans have nothing to do with that.

Summarizing, the science of climate change has become politically controversial, and there are diametrically opposite interpretations of the same climatic events. Multiple lines of evidence point to changes in climate over the last 150 years. Debate continues, however, on what is causing changes in the temperature and precipitation patterns since the late nineteenth century the changes in atmospheric chemistry due to human activities could lead to warming (due to GHG) or cooling (due to aerosols), which seems to explain a large part of the surface temperature oscillations at a short-term scale. The IPCC 2013 report in line with its earlier deductions emphasized that *"It is extremely likely that more than half of the observed increase in global average surface temperature from 1951 to 2010 was caused by the anthropogenic increase in greenhouse gas concentrations and other anthropogenic forcings together"* (in the IPCC report the term "extremely likely" corresponds to 95 % probability). Note that the above probability estimate marks a sharp increase in the IPCC's confidence level compared to its 2007 and 2001 reports, where it was 90 % and 66 %, respectively, confident of the similar conclusion. More than 850 experts and 50 editors from 85 countries have contributed to the 2013 report, which underscores the significance of the main conclusions of the report.

Although the ever-increasing body of evidence points to the human imprint in the current climate change trend, it is not the intent of this book to revisit the range of views with regard to the ongoing heated "climate debate," or some purported controversies surrounding the climate change science and the IPCC reports. There are many excellent books and reviews dedicated to this topic. [1]

4.2. Effect of Threat of Global Warming

There is now consensus among scientists that the temperature of the Earth is increasing and that carbon dioxide in the atmosphere is increasing. There is suspicion that the increase in carbon dioxide is from the burning of fossil fuels and that this is promoting the increase in temperature, along with other greenhouse gases, such as methane, nitrous oxide, and gaseous fluorocarbons. However, others argue that this could be part of a normal cycle of the Earth, not affected much by man. Certainly, the warming of oceans promotes the frequency of hurricanes and typhoons as has taken their toll in 2004 and 2005. How much should we reduce the burning of fossil fuels, including petroleum, because of the fear of causing global warming? Too tight a restriction

---

[1]Nazim Muradov: Liberating Energy from Carbon: Introduction to Decarbonization. Springer Science+Business Media New York 2014. P 25: 30

on the use of fossil fuels would cause the economy to contract, but in 2005 the United States observed the strong negative impact on their economy and human lives caused by hurricanes.

We cannot ignore the possibility that unless the use of fossil fuels is reduced, the Earth will continue to get warmer and hurricanes will continue to be more frequent and more severe.

The 1997 Kyoto Protocol was an attempt to reach an agreement among nations to reduce the emissions of greenhouse gases. Upon ratification by Russia (of the agreement reached for reduction by 55% of the carbon dioxide emissions in 1990 by countries included in Annex I) on November 18, 2004, this agreement came in force on February 16, 2005. By 2006, a total of 162 nations have ratified the agreement, with the notable exceptions of the United States and Australia.

Under the agreement, by 2010, industrialized nations will reduce the total emissions of greenhouse gases by 5.2% of that in 1990. The reduction requirements vary with country. For example, the reductions required by the European Union is 8%, by the United States is 7%, by Japan is 6%, and by Russia is 0%.

Australia is permitted an 8% increase. Because China and India are not included among the Annex I countries, they are exempt from any restrictions, despite China being the country with the second largest emission of greenhouse gases. However, on a per person basis, the emissions of greenhouse gases by China and India are among the smallest in the world. Although many claims that the Kyoto Protocol does not go far enough, the United States, the largest emitter of greenhouse gases, refuses to sign because it feels the degree of reduction is unfair relative to other countries and that such a reduction will harm its economy.

Whatever the status of the agreement on the Kyoto Protocol, it is clear that the United States needs to move in the direction of reducing carbon dioxide emissions as opposed to the continued increase that we have come to expect. The first reductions should be those that are positive for both our economy and the environment.

We have already discussed the need to conserve the use of petroleum derived fuels for vehicles. This has the positive side effect of reducing carbon dioxide emissions. The manufacture of biofuels, such as ethanol, butanol, and biodiesel, promises to consume as much carbon dioxide by agricultural growth as produced from combustion as long as fossil fuels are not used for refining them.

Electrical power generation is the industry with by far the greatest carbon dioxide emissions. We already need to burn more natural gas than coal to reduce emissions of gases that cause acid rain, and sulfur and nitrogen oxides. This switch has the added feature of a reduction in carbon dioxide emissions because methane combustion produces more water vapor relative to carbon dioxide than the combustion of coal. An increase in electrical power generation from nuclear, water power, solar, and wind sources is even better as they produce no carbon dioxide or acid rain.

Petroleum refining is the industry with the second largest emission of carbon dioxide, and energy is second only to crude oil among direct costs to refineries.

Therefore, refineries have the opportunity to reduce substantially their operating costs and the emission of carbon dioxide at the same time. One method is to optimize the heat exchanger network in the refinery. Another method is to mitigate the fouling of heat exchangers and fired heaters. Foulants cause energy loss by forming insulating layers on heat exchange surfaces. Fouling mitigation has the extra benefit of extending the period between refinery shutdowns for maintenance, thereby increasing the effective refinery capacity.

Carbon dioxide can be absorbed out of power plants or refinery smokestacks, liquefied, and pumped into oil wells to increase the recovery of oil (secondary oil recovery). About half the carbon dioxide injected remains within the formation.

Therefore, carbon dioxide flooding, with increased petroleum production, is the most economical way to sequester carbon dioxide. Unfortunately, power plants are normally not located near petroleum production sites. The alternatives are pipelining carbon dioxide to petroleum production sites or sequestering the carbon dioxide as a supercritical gas in deep saline reservoirs (CCS, carbon capture and sequestration). In addition, there is not enough petroleum reservoir volume in the United States to contain all the carbon dioxide from the burning of fossil fuels at power plants and refineries. The good news is that there are no technical hurdles to widespread CCS. Of course, the consumer will have to pay much more for energy, but if introduced gradually, the economy will not collapse.

Technological advances should even cushion the economic impact, taking advantage of the advanced tools of petroleum engineers and geologists. Canada is already moving to CCS to reduce the impact of exploiting the tar sands in Alberta on greenhouse gas emissions. Meanwhile, the United States is waiting for new public policy and legislation by a more enlightened government and public. [1]

4.3. Measuring the Impact of Regulatory Announcements on CO2 Returns

In order to measure the impact of different announcements on carbon returns, an event study technique is applied. If a market is efficient, new information will be reflected in asset prices as it becomes available. Therefore, the significance of an event can be assessed by observing the magnitude of the price changes around the time of the announcement. much of the research on the carbon market so far has relied on the use of a constant mean return model as a benchmark against which abnormal returns are estimated. This model assumes that the asset's returns are normally distributed with a time-invariant mean and variance. The underlying premise is that future observations

---

([1])Irwin A. Wiehe: Process Chemistry of Petroleum Macromolecules. Taylor & Francis Group, LLC. 2008. P 9:11

will be drawn from the same distribution. To address the high frequency of unscheduled information releases on the market, authors have adjusted the model by trimming the highest and lowest values of the mean carbon return over the estimation period. The disadvantage of the constant mean return model is that it does not control for changes in energy prices, extreme weather events and economic activity. Thus, abnormal return estimates may be overstated.

Abnormal returns associated with the various types of events are calculated with the following regression: [1]

$$R_{carbon,t} = \alpha_0 + \sum_{j=1}^{n} \beta_j D_{j,t} + \varepsilon_t$$

where $R_{carbon;t}$ is the continuously compounded rate of return for carbon futures on day t. $D_{j,t}$ is a dummy variable equal to 1 on the event day and 0 otherwise for all j = 1, 2, ..., n subcategories of events. The intercept x_0 represents the mean daily log return of carbon during non-event days. The regression coefficients of the event dummies B_j are the calculated mean abnormal returns related to the

---

[1] Yulia Veld-Merkoulova • Svetlana Viteva: Carbon Finance. Springer International Publishing Switzerland 2016. P 28

specific events. In other words, they are the daily differences from the mean carbon returns over the non-event days.

The model is estimated for the 1595 trading days over the period 22/04/2005 to 30/06/2011. The sample is broken down in two ways: (1) building on earlier work, we use the financial crisis to divide the sample, and (2) we use a structural test to detect breaks in the time series of the carbon returns. Two different methodologies are employed to prevent arbitrary choices of subsamples and to provide a test of robustness for the results.

A multifactor model can control for market-wide developments and exogenous influences on the carbon prices. We rely heavily on the existing literature in choosing fossil fuel prices, economic indicators and temperature as explanatory variables in the model. The prices of natural gas directly affect carbon prices as power plants switch to carbon-intensive coal-fired electricity generation when gas prices rise. With gas futures prices largely derived from oil prices, oil is another key driver for carbon. Strong economic activity also translates into higher EUA prices as companies produce more and emit more carbon in order to meet the higher demand for their goods. Extreme weather indirectly affects carbon prices through its impact on energy demand. The multifactor regression model takes on the following form: [1]

$$R_{carbon,t} = z_0 + \theta_{oil}R_{oil,t} + \theta_{gas}R_{gas,t} + \theta_{equity}R_{equity,t} + \theta_{cold}D_{cold,t} + \theta_{hot}D_{hot,t} + \sum_{j=1}^{n} \beta_j D_{j,t} + \varepsilon_t$$

where $R_{carbon;t}=R_{oil;t}=R_{gas;t}=R_{equity;t}$ is the continuously compounded rate of return for carbon/oil/gas/stock market on day t. D_{hot} and D_{cold} are dummy variables which take on the values of 1 on extremely hot and cold days and 0 otherwise.

The main assumption underlying OLS analysis is that the regressors are exogenous to the dependent variable. To prevent an endogeneity problem, we limit the use of mutually interactive regressors in this Eq. For example, electricity is often quoted as a carbon price driver. We capture its impact on carbon using extreme weather events since it is through the demand for electricity that temperature affects EUA prices. Some researchers have used clean dark and spark spreads as well as the fuel switching EUA price in addition to the absolute

---

[1]Yulia Veld-Merkoulova • Svetlana Viteva: Carbon Finance. Springer International Publishing Switzerland 2016. P 28: 29

prices of fossil fuels as carbon price drivers. In addition to our concerns about introducing such correlated variables in the analysis, we question the relevance of these variables as EUA price determinants altogether. For instance, a switch between energy generation sources may occur even though carbon price may be below its "switch" level, if energy demand is so high that both coal- and gas-fired units need to be running to meet the demand. A problem with the use of spreads as carbon price drivers is that due to their different efficiencies, power plants will switch from coal- to gas-fired units at different EUA prices. The clean spreads used in most studies rely on assumptions about the average plant size and the average plant efficiency and grossly over-simplify the analysis by assuming homogenous plants across countries. [1]

4.4. Does CO2 Emissions Performance Matter for Stock Prices?

Investors are becoming increasingly concerned with the non-financial aspects of a company's behavior, such as the impact of its operations and products on the environment. Investment management companies have launched funds with environmental remits in response to the growing demand for ethical and

---

[1] Yulia Veld-Merkoulova • Svetlana Viteva: Carbon Finance. Springer International Publishing Switzerland 2016. P 29: 30

green businesses. There are so-called dark green funds, such as Kames Capital Ethical Equity, which do not invest in companies whose activities are judged to be environmentally unsound or are "in energy intensive industries which are not tackling the issue of climate change. Europe's commercial banks have also recognized the problem of climate change and have introduced policies to exert pressure on polluters which emit high levels of carbon into the atmosphere. HSBC, Standard Chartered, BNP Paribas and Credit Agricole have adopted new standards for the financing of coal-fired power plants, whereby dirty plants with emissions intensities above a certain threshold will not qualify for financing. Companies themselves have begun to implement measures to reduce their carbon footprint—from energy consumption savings to procurement of electricity for the firm's own energy use from renewable sources. Some firms, National Grid being one example, even offer monetary rewards to executives and environmental managers for successful achievement of internally set up emissions reduction targets. As awareness of climate change has seemingly gained momentum in society at large, one could argue that the carbon performance of companies should become a standard component of investment analysis. [1]

---

[1]Yulia Veld-Merkoulova • Svetlana Viteva: Carbon Finance. Springer International Publishing Switzerland

Significant market reactions to the verified emissions data disclosures are found in only one out of the six verification events over the period 2005–2011 which suggests that investors do not perceive carbon performance as important enough to be priced into firm valuations yet. The level of freely allocated allowances and actual emissions during the year are shown to be insignificant in explaining the observed stock price responses. We find some support for the hypothesis that the emissions reports lead to a stronger market reaction in companies with high carbon-intensive activities. No statistically significant proof is found that the market reacts differently towards environmental leaders and laggards upon disclosure of their carbon emissions data. Corporate carbon performance does not seem to be affected by the publication of emissions reports either. We conclude that, as it stands today, the EU ETS is not meeting the socially desirable objective of promoting the transition to a low-carbon economy. [1]

Several studies report a significant relationship between carbon prices and the stock prices of ETS-covered companies, particularly for power companies. While the scheme has had

---

2016. P 79: 80
[1]Yulia Veld-Merkoulova • Svetlana Viteva: Carbon Finance. Springer International Publishing Switzerland 2016. P 81

a limited impact on the cost structure of power companies because of generous-free EUA allocations, electricity companies have overcompensated for the opportunity cost of carbon by raising electricity prices more than proportionately and earning regulatory rents. Because energy producers operate in generally isolated domestic markets, it makes it relatively easy for them to pass on the carbon costs to their customers. While there is no consensus over the exact role, the electricity market structure plays in determining the degree of cost pass-through; there is strong evidence of electricity price increases to incorporate the price of carbon. For energy-intensive companies, this means that in addition to the direct costs of buying allowances and/or reducing their carbon footprint, they also have the indirect costs of higher electricity bills. [1]

Oberndorfer (2009) models the returns of an equally weighted portfolio made up of the 11 largest publicly traded European electricity producers as a function of the broad market, carbon, electricity and fuel prices. The author emphasizes the importance of using oil and gas as explanatory variables because of their dual role as price drivers for both energy stocks and carbon allowances. A time- and country-specific

---

[1] Yulia Veld-Merkoulova • Svetlana Viteva: Carbon Finance. Springer International Publishing Switzerland 2016. P 83: 84

statistically significant positive association between the returns of power companies and carbon is reported. Veith et al. (2009) examine 22 large European electricity producers, not all of which are regulated by the ETS, and confirm Oberndorfer's (2009) conclusion that stock prices have been positively associated with carbon prices during Phase I. The returns of power companies are modelled as a function of the market portfolio and carbon only but the findings are shown to be robust to the addition of oil, gas, the electricity market structure and its regulatory framework as independent variables. However, the estimated positive correlation between the prices of power companies and carbon breaks down when the proportion of fossil electricity generation is accounted for. [1]

Lastly, Bushnell et al. (2013) relate the returns of carbon certificates and ETS-covered companies in an event study. The stock prices of 90 companies across various industries are examined following the sharp drop of the carbon price on April 25, 2006 when information was leaked prior to the first official disclosure of emissions data by the EC. A statistically significant positive link between carbon prices and stock prices of covered entities is reported for both carbon-intensive companies as well as

---

[1] Yulia Veld-Merkoulova • Svetlana Viteva: Carbon Finance. Springer International Publishing Switzerland 2016. P 84

energy-intensive companies with little exposure to international trade. Abnormal returns are estimated as parameterized dummy coefficients in an ordinary least squares framework. The return-generating model, however, employs the broad market as the only source of priced risk, possibly producing abnormal return estimates which may be driven by an omitted risk factor. [1]

4.5. Information Assimilation in the European Carbon Market

The preponderance of the EU ETS literature has focused on market operating and pricing mechanisms, and the economic impact of the EU ETS market, whereas only a small number of the published articles have studied transaction level information assimilation in this market. Indeed, previous related work, largely focuses on the announcement effects on returns, with only indirectly related studies of the volatility, spread and trading volume issues, evident in the literature. [2]

The exceptions include Chevallier (2009), Rittler (2012), Conrad et al. (2012),

---

[1] Yulia Veld-Merkoulova • Svetlana Viteva: Carbon Finance. Springer International Publishing Switzerland 2016. P 84

[2] Andre´ Dorsman • O¨ zgЄur Arslan-Ayaydin • Mehmet Baha Karan: Energy and Finance. Springer International Publishing Switzerland 2016. P 15

Bredin et al. (2014) and Bredin et al. (2016). Conrad et al. (2012) studied high frequency data with a view to examining the impact of the European Commission's second National Allocation Plan (NAP) as well as a set of scheduled macroeconomic news on the EUA Futures returns from 2006 to 2010. An especially important exception to the dearth of contributions to the literature on information assimilation at high frequency around publicly scheduled announcements, in the European carbon market, is the study by Conrad et al. (2012). Conrad et al. (2012) report that several of their scheduled announcements influence EUA futures returns immediately or within several minutes subsequent to the announcements. They show, accounting for intra-day periodicity, volatility clustering and volatility persistence, that EUA prices do respond to good news in regard to current and expected economic activity in Germany and the United States. They also find that European Commission decisions on second National Allocation Plans have a strong and immediate impact on EUA prices. In a similar vein, Mizrach and Otsubo (2014) show that realized volatility, bid ask spreads and adverse selection costs decline with verified emission releases in April, which is indicative of information assimilation at these announcements. [1]

---

[1] Andre´ Dorsman • O¨ zg€ur Arslan-Ayaydin • Mehmet Baha Karan: Energy and Finance. Springer International

Turning to the types of agents evident in the market, Kalaitzoglou and Ibrahim (2013) study transaction-by-transaction December 2008 expiration futures data. They find that informed, fundamental and uninformed traders prevail in the EU ETS, with faster reactions from fundamental traders in Phase II. Bredin et al. (2014) show that accounting for duration between trades there is a negative contemporaneous volume volatility relation in the EU ETS futures market on December 2005 to December 2012 expiration contracts. This finding suggests a predominance of liquidity (uninformed) traders in the market. Nevertheless, Mizrach and Otsubo (2014) provide evidence of strategic trading by informed institutional traders (positively autocorrelated trade direction, short time intervals between trades and a large adverse selection component of the bid-ask spreads). This result indicates, as in well traded capital markets (Fleming and Remolona 1999; Balduzzi et al. 2001; Green 2004; Riordan et al. 2013), a potential for a period of information asymmetry across agent types after informative announcements. Informed and fundamental traders may thus communicate their insight by their trading decisions and thus influence the information assimilation process related to publicly scheduled announcements. [1]

Publishing Switzerland 2016. P 15: 16
[1]Andre´ Dorsman • O¨ zg€ur Arslan-Ayaydin • Mehmet

The quality of EU ETS price signals has been a focus of controversy in respect to the light shed by these signals on the functioning of the European carbon market. In the Kyoto Phase of the EU ETS the price signals tumbled quite dramatically, however, European economies had been on a low or negative economic growth path during this time and the costs associated with emissions reductions should reflect the economic conditions. Indeed, Article 1 of the EU ETS Directive states that the objective of the scheme is to "promote reductions of greenhouse gas in a cost-effective and economically efficient manner" (Page 6). As a result, price signals are not necessarily a reflection of the quality of functioning of the emissions trading system. Instead, we propose that tests concerning how well the market assimilates new information should be of paramount importance. [1]

The concept of a price on greenhouse emissions has a compelling logic; all other things being equal, a price on carbon will reduce carbon relative to other economic indicators. The European experience with carbon taxes since the 1990s has been that carbon taxes do in fact reduce emissions from what they would

---

Baha Karan: Energy and Finance. Springer International Publishing Switzerland 2016. P 16

([1])Andre′ Dorsman • O″ zg€ur Arslan-Ayaydin • Mehmet Baha Karan: Energy and Finance. Springer International Publishing Switzerland 2016. P 25

have otherwise been, and mostly without a significant loss of industrial competitiveness. Indeed, even putting aside the issue of climate change, there is an argument that shifting the tax burden from income taxes in favor of consumption taxes will tend to encourage savings and investment. [1]

But unlike the pricing of social ills or pollutants, the purpose here is not just to marginally reduce the quantity of emissions, but change, in a fundamental way, the energy systems that *enable* the advanced societies, along with the health, education, industry, and culture that is modernity.

There is little argument against renewable energy providing an abatement role within a fossil-fueled economy; indeed, carbon pricing is likely to be an effective marginal *abatement* strategy in the advanced economies. But it is less clear that it can be an effective global *energy* strategy in an era of lowering energy return on investment and the need to bring affordable energy to much of world's population. A discussion of the role of carbon pricing provides an opportunity to draw out some of the challenges of shifting to a high-

---

[1] Graham Palmer: Energy in Australia. Springer Cham Heidelberg New York Dordrecht London 2014. P 71

penetration renewables scenario within a global context. [1]

---

[1] Graham Palmer: Energy in Australia. Springer Cham Heidelberg New York Dordrecht London 2014. P 71

5. Carbon Taxation

But there is a further problem with a rising carbon price. Tol (2012) defined the "Leviathan tax" as the hypothetical short-run maximum carbon tax that is budget neutral (i.e. all other taxes are reduced to zero and replaced by a carbon tax). The Leviathan tax is calculated from the CO_2 emissions, CO_2 intensity of the economy, and the total tax revenue for the country, excluding taxes that directly finance social security programs.

For developed countries such as Australia, the United Kingdom, and the United States, the short-run theoretical Leviathan tax can be above $200 per ton CO_2 since the advanced nations collect substantial taxes and also generate substantial economic activity per unit of energy, even if the energy is based on high-emission fuels. Hence, the Leviathan tax does not pose a fundamental constraint on the short-run carbon price for these countries.

On the other hand, a $1-per-tonne carbon could fund the entire government budgets of Nigeria and Liberia. In the case of the first, third, and fourth highest emitting countries, China, Russia, and India, the Leviathan tax has been calculated by Tol using 2005 data as $29, $36, and $45, respectively (USD 2000). [1]

The first attempt to introduce a common framework for EU carbon and energy taxation occurred as far back as 1992 (COM/92/226), but neither it nor its amended proposal achieved significant success. According to the 1992 proposal, excise rates should reflect both carbon and energy content of the taxed fuels. In 1997 such an approach was abandoned and the draft directive called for a staggered introduction of minimum tax rates on all energy products (COM/97/30). Policy guidelines also specified exemptions, reductions and tax refunds for specific sectors and uses. Still, the proposal faced hard opposition, and no consensus could be reached, due—among others —to concerns about potential adverse impacts on EU industrial competitiveness.

After no major progress in 1999 and 2000, an agreement on EU-wide minimum energy tax levels was scheduled to be reached by the end of 2002. Conflicting opinions from a number of countries caused a series of postponements. Finally, in October 2003 the agreement on the text of a directive was achieved. The "Directive restructuring the Community framework for the taxation of energy products and electricity" replaced its

---

([1])Graham Palmer: Energy in Australia. Springer Cham Heidelberg New York Dordrecht London 2014. P 78

1992 predecessor which dealt just with mineral oils.

The Directive 2003/96/EC set minimum rates for all energy products, including natural gas and solid fuels, as well as electricity. The Directive is intended to reduce distortions of competition, both between Member States created by divergent rates of tax on energy products, and between mineral oils and the other energy products. It is also intended to increase incentives to use energy more efficiently. The Directive sets common taxation rules for a range of fuels, including many oil products, coal and natural gas, and for electricity consumption. For each, it sets a minimum level of tax expressed in terms of the volume, weight, or energy content of the fuel. The directive also sets out transitional measures and permitted derogations (both general and country-specific) from the minimum levels, such as exemptions for particular sectors. [1]

5.1. TAX SPINNING

The first activity of the crude oil producers of the United Kingdom was to optimize the taxation burden (tax spinning). The taxes due to the department of Inland Revenue

---

[1] Rossella Bardazzi • Maria Grazia Pazienza Alberto Tonini: European Energy and Climate Security. Springer International Publishing Switzerland 2016. P 240: 241

were set as a fixed percentage (40–50%) of the value of each single cargo. The lower the price, the lower the taxes to be paid. The price had to be advised by each producer within 48 hours from completion of loading. This allowed the producing companies, in the two days following the loading, to intensify their trading operations on physical cargoes, and to attribute the lowest of the prices obtained to the cargo just taken and to declare it to the Inland Revenue with evident and sizeable tax advantages. This practice was tolerated by the British authorities, as a form of incentive to invest in offshore activities. Recent years have, however, seen limitations and restrictions being gradually imposed on this tax flexibility, forcing companies operating in the UK to pay taxes corresponding to the prices actually obtained. [1]

5.2. Corporate income tax

Income tax systems usually consist of a basic, single rate structure, plus provisions for deduction of all costs items from the tax base, sometimes with supplementary levies and tax incentives. The overall level of corporate income tax rates varies considerably from country to country. In many countries the level is typically between 25 per cent and 35 per cent.

---

[1]Salvatore Carollo: Understanding Oil Prices A John Wiley & Sons, Ltd., Publication. 2012. P 105

Most countries provide an incentive for exploration and development by allowing exploration costs to be recovered immediately and allowing accelerated recovery of development costs (tax depreciation), for example, over five years or less. Accelerated depreciation brings forward payback for the investor and reduces the latter's cumulative cash exposure. In addition to cost deductions, in many cases interest expenses and losses carried forward and/or back are commonly allowed in the computation of the tax liability. All forms of income tax allow relief for capital expenditure (at a varying pace), but extra reliefs are sometimes given to provide incentives to develop high cost 'marginal' projects.

The UK has gone further than most and introduced 100 per cent depreciation in the year of expenditure. This ensures that no project will pay tax until payback has been secured – a uniquely attractive feature for investors.

The income tax regime for oil and gas companies is generally the same regime that applies to all corporate activities for all industries in the country in question. Though the rate may be higher and the range of qualifying cost deductions may differ (so that some ring-fencing is needed), the tax is levied at a corporate rather than oil field level, as such it is generally known as corporation tax or tax on corporate net income. Since income tax is a profit-based tax, it introduces fewer distortions compared to an over-reliance on revenue-based taxes. [1]

5.3. Special petroleum tax

Many concessionary regimes also include a special petroleum tax, similar to a resource rent tax, in order to capture a larger share of economic rent from oil production. The special tax is usually imposed along with the general corporate income tax but it is levied on a project or field basis rather than on aggregate company income. The tax is normally based on cash flow but is imposed only when cumulative cash flow is positive. Negative cash flows are carried forward and deducted from positive cash flows in later periods. The negative net cash flows may be uplifted by a minimum rate of return requirement and added to the next year's net cash flow. The uplift is often characterized as a proxy for financing costs. The accumulation process is continued until a positive net cash flow is generated. No special tax is payable until the firm has recovered its costs inclusive of a threshold rate of return which is compounded from year to year. Tax kicks in only when

---

[1]Philip Daniel, Michael Keen and Charles McPherson: The Taxation of Petroleum and Minerals. international Monetary Fund. 2010. P 96

positive cash flows emerge, the project investment is recovered and a threshold return on the investment is made. If costs rise or oil prices fall, taxable profits change in sympathy, as does the special petroleum tax burden. Incremental investment opportunities may be attractive in fields with existing production and current taxable income. In this case, the investment will typically secure immediate or accelerated tax relief in comparison to a greenfield or standalone opportunity where there is a greater time lag between the investment and the tax relief. Also, if the investment is unproductive the tax relief is still available which cushions the impact on the investor. [1]

5.4. Additional payments and measures

Other payments can also be made to the government in oil producing countries where concessionary regimes apply. These include bonuses, which are lump sum payments made to the government (and are also common under contractual systems). They can be signature or lease bonus, payable upon signing the agreement with the government or award of a lease, discovery bonus, payable when a commercial discovery is made, or production bonus, payable at an agreed amount (or bid) upon the

---

[1] Philip Daniel, Michael Keen and Charles McPherson: The Taxation of Petroleum and Minerals. international Monetary Fund. 2010. P 96: 97

achievement of a stated level of daily production.

Signature bonuses capture some of the anticipated resource value regardless of the success of exploration and production activities. Since the investment is made up-front, once paid, they have no further impact on the future economic decisions of the investor. The sums can be very large; they comprise a material proportion of overall government take, particularly if the acreage is unproductive.

The discovery bonus is also a one-off fee. It is required after commercial discovery is declared and after the NOC has approved the IOCs development plan. Production bonuses, however, can be recurring. They are due when production reaches a certain level. They are normally on a sliding scale of production, therefore if daily production reaches a certain level the government takes a fixed sum, which increases if daily production reaches higher levels. Depending on the tax regime, bonuses may be deductible for income tax purposes.

Some countries ring-fence their oil and gas activities (usually under corporate income tax) whilst others ring-fence individual projects (usually under special petroleum tax). Ring-fencing imposes a limitation on deductions for tax purposes across different activities or projects undertaken by the same taxpayer. In other words, all costs associated with a given license or field must be deducted from revenues generated within that field – not from other licenses or fields.

These rules matter for two main reasons. First, the absence of ring-fencing Can postpone government tax receipts because a company that undertakes a series of projects is able to deduct exploration and development costs from each new project against the income of projects that are already generating taxable income.

Second, as an oil and gas area mature, the absence of ring-fencing may discriminate against new entrants that have no income against which to deduct exploration or development expenditures. However, existing players are encouraged to sustain their investment given the availability of the tax shelter. [1]

5.5. Natural gas taxation

The fiscal regimes for upstream and midstream operations are very different in most

---

[1] Philip Daniel, Michael Keen and Charles McPherson: The Taxation of Petroleum and Minerals. international Monetary Fund. 2010. P 97: 98

producing countries. Upstream production tends to be subject to more complex fiscal terms and can include bonuses, royalty, production sharing and windfall profits taxes, as well as corporate/petroleum income tax. Midstream operations, on the other hand, tend to be treated as general industrial projects and are subject only to standard corporate income tax. Major projects, such as greenfield LNG plants, may even receive fiscal incentives such as temporary tax holidays.

The Malaysian LNG (MLNG) project highlights the differences between midstream and upstream taxation policies and the implications for other government policies, such as gas pricing and equity participation. Figure 6.6 illustrates the

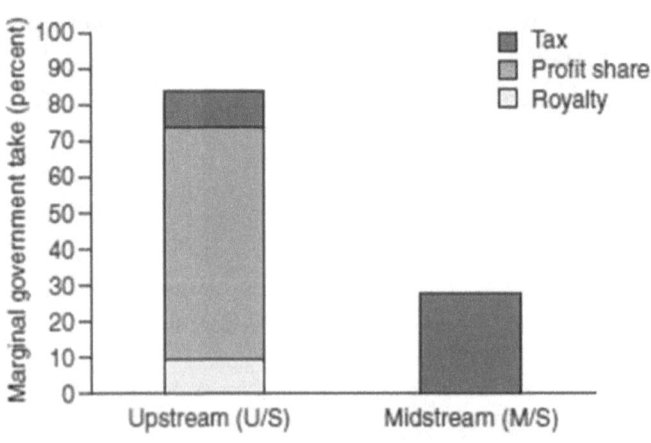

significant difference in the government take1 from Malaysian upstream and midstream operations, where the total fiscal take is 83 per cent of upstream profits but only 28 per cent of midstream profits.

Petronas, the Malaysian national oil company (NOC), has a 50:50 joint venture with Shell in the upstream MLNG PSC. Petronas is also the purchaser of the gas at the plant gate, where it then sells the gas on to the LNG plant owners (at the same price as it pays for the gas). The price at the plant gate is usually referred to as the 'gas transfer price'. Petronas owns 90 per cent of the plant, which sells LNG to markets in North Asia.

The relationship between fiscal and gas pricing policies is critical. Figure 6.7 illustrates the difference between the total government take and investor profits from the project, under three different transfer pricing policies:

• Transfer price is established at the maximum price the midstream can pay (i.e. the plant's breakeven price).

• Transfer price is established at the minimum price the upstream can receive (i.e. the producer's breakeven price).

• Transfer price is established at the midpoint between upstream and midstream breakeven prices.

The Figure shows the distribution of the project's total profit, i.e. LNG price less the upstream and midstream costs.

The 'midstream breakeven' policy (which is comparable to the Indonesian policy of only reimbursing the LNG plant's costs) ensures that the upstream transfer/netback price is as high as possible. Figure 6.7 shows that, under these assumptions, this policy generates the highest level of overall government take because of the higher fiscal take from upstream operations.

The 'upstream breakeven' policy, which results in all of the economic rent residing in the midstream operation, is far less common. It is comparable to the

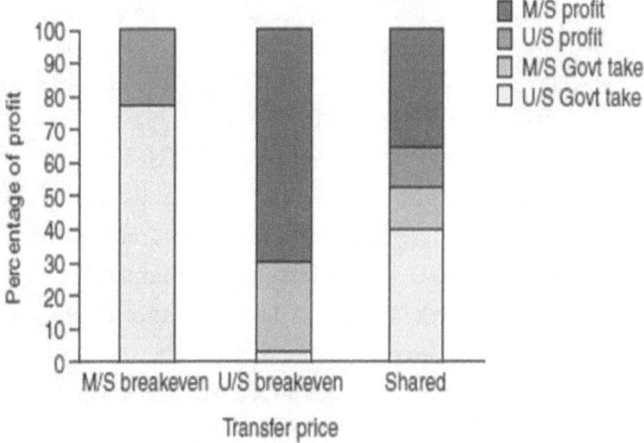

situation where upstream producers are deemed to have no rights to gas associated with oil production and deliver the gas to the government or midstream plant, with only costs reimbursed (e.g. Oman LNG) or recovered from oil revenues (e.g. Angola LNG). As a result of the lower tax rates applicable to the midstream operation, this generates the lowest overall government take of the different options.

The third alternative is that the difference between the two breakeven prices is shared between the upstream and midstream operations, either as a result of negotiation between the two parties or by government regulation. This results in a government take from the total project somewhere between the two extremes.

An example of this system is Australia's residual price mechanism (RPM), which is established for integrated LNG projects. (See Figure 6.8.) Australia levies a Petroleum Resource Rent Tax (PRRT) on upstream profits, but not on midstream operations. If there is no arm's-length agreement between the two operations, or a comparable local benchmark or price formula agreed in advance with government, then a proxy gas transfer price (GTP) needs to be established for purposes of calculating the PRRT payable by the upstream operation. Under the RPM, two prices are established:

• Cost-plus price.

• Netback price.

The RPM involves taking the average of the gap (or economic rent) between the cost-plus and netback prices for that operation. The cost-plus price represents the lowest price the upstream phase of a gas to liquids operation would sell its sales gas for; that is, the lowest price at which that operation would fully recover its costs of producing the sales gas. A gas transfer price below the cost-plus price means that it would be uneconomic to produce sales gas.

The netback price represents the highest price the midstream phase of a gas to liquids operation would pay for sales gas; that is, the highest price the operation

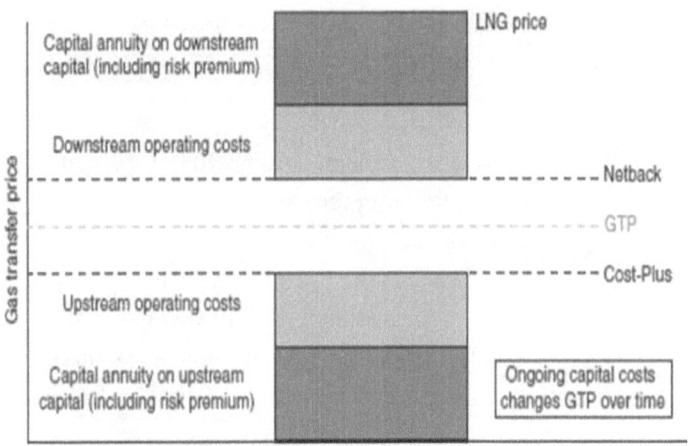

could pay for sales gas and fully recover its costs of using the sales gas to produce LNG from the proceeds the operation obtains from selling LNG in the market place. A gas transfer price above the netback price means that it would be uneconomic to produce LNG.

In the cost-plus and netback calculations, capital costs incurred in the project pre-first gas are augmented using a capital allowance. Capital costs are uplifted by the long-term bond-rate plus a 'risk premium' of 7 per cent.

A feature of the RPM is that the transfer price tends to rise throughout the life of the project – a function of greater ongoing capital expenditure in the upstream phase of the project. This has the effect of gradually shifting more of the revenue to the upstream (higher tax) phase, and steadily increases the overall tax burden on the project.

As a general rule, therefore, the government will prefer to see the upstream transfer price as high as possible when the upstream fiscal take is higher than from midstream operations. However, the government's equity interest in the chain's links can alter this perception. In the Malaysian LNG project example, the overall country takes – i.e. the government take plus the NOC's equity interest – can be calculated and compared with the other companies' profit under the different pricing policies.

The Figure shows that the very high equity interest in the lower-taxed midstream operation results in a higher overall 'country take' when the lowest upstream transfer price is used than when the upstream transfer price is highest.

As long as the government regards fiscal revenue and the NOC profits as similar sources of revenue, its attitude to transfer pricing can, therefore, be completely changed as a result of the difference in the NOC equity interest in the different links of the chain. Issues arise, however, when the NOC's profits begin to be diverted away from government coffers – for example, in the expansion of international investments or in dividend payments following part-privatization.

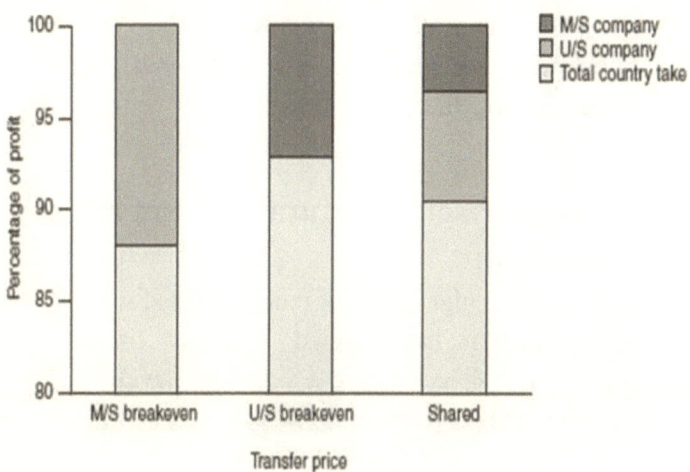

Thus, three policies relating to segmented natural gas projects need to be developed simultaneously:

i Transfer pricing.

ii NOC equity in different links in the chain.

iii Upstream and midstream fiscal terms.

One route to resolving these simultaneous issues is to integrate the upstream and midstream operations into a single project with a specific fiscal regime. The NOC can take an equity interest in the entire project and there would be no need for an upstream transfer price as all fiscal considerations will be based on the final price received and all costs will be considered together. [1]

5.6. Comparison of natural gas and oil taxation

The high levels of rent associated with oil production has resulted in many fiscal regimes for oil generating a very high level of government take from oil revenues.

Some governments have used the existence of highly profitable oil projects to incentivize development of less attractive gas projects, particularly associated gas. Gas which cannot be produced commercially must either be

---

[1]Philip Daniel, Michael Keen and Charles McPherson: The Taxation of Petroleum and Minerals. international Monetary Fund. 2010. P 169: 173

re-injected or flared. If the quantities of gas are large, re-injection can only be a temporary solution and gas flaring is universally discouraged (even if it still continues in some old facilities). Investors and government keen to progress development of oil then need to seek alternative solutions for the simultaneous development of the gas.

Some examples of the resolution of this apparent stalemate can be found in:

• Nigeria: oil producers are currently allowed to include costs associated with the development of gas facilities in the capital cost pool for oil tax purposes and, therefore, receive tax relief at the Petroleum Profits Tax (PPT) rate of 85 per cent. Any operating profit from the gas sales (i.e. revenue less operating costs) is only liable to standard corporate income tax at 30 per cent. This enables producers to accept much lower gas prices than would be possible if the gas capital costs were not consolidated with oil.

• Angola: the NOC receives associated gas from certain Deepwater oil developments free of charge at the beach. In return the oil producers are allowed to include the costs of the gas pipeline in their cost recovery pool, which attracts an uplift allowance and is included in the IRR-based oil production-sharing calculation, thus reducing the government's share of the oil profits.

• Algeria: in some projects, the investor is entitled to a share of the proceeds from sales of condensate and other associated liquids to recover costs and make a return, but all of the separated gas production is taken by the national oil company, Sonatrach.

Governments also often compensate for the less attractive economics of gas projects by offering more attractive fiscal terms to gas producers, compared to oil. These can take several forms, but the most common are:

• lower royalty rates (e.g. Nigeria, Tunisia, Vietnam);

• higher cost-recovery ceilings and/or profit shares (e.g. Egypt, Indonesia, Malaysia);

• lower tax rates (e.g. Nigeria, Tunisia, Papua New Guinea); and

• exemption from certain oil taxes (e.g. Trinidad and Tobago (Supplementary Petroleum Tax)).

Just as gas can be a by-product of oil production, liquids may also be present in gas production streams (i.e. condensate or natural gas liquids (NGLs)). If the fiscal terms for oil and gas are differentiated, the treatment of condensate and other liquids produced in association with gas is an important issue for policy makers. On one hand, as condensate tends to command prices comparable to oil, it is logical for these revenues to be treated as oil revenue and subject to the same fiscal terms as oil. This is the practice followed in most countries.

On the other hand, treating the liquids revenue as gas revenue and subjecting these revenues to lower tax rates can significantly increase the economic viability of a gas project and enable the 'breakeven' gas price required to be much lower than if there were no associated liquids. If a very high level of tax is levied on the liquids revenue, however, this economic advantage is eroded for investors. This issue is most complex when the gas production is associated with oil production. With facilities already established for the export of oil, it makes sense to separate any liquids associated with gas production in the upstream facilities and export these using the oil infrastructure. It is then more difficult for investors to argue for preferential fiscal treatment for the condensate revenues.

The application of differentiated fiscal terms when oil and gas are produced together requires costs to be allocated to the different revenue streams. Many costs, particularly operating and maintenance costs, will be common to both operations and impossible to identify as pertaining to one or the other. In these situations, some form of cost allocation is required, which can be problematic and open to possible manipulation by investors to minimize the fiscal take. The most common approach is to allocate shared costs each year according to the proportion of total revenue generated by the project which is attributable to the different production streams.

In the few areas where domestic gas prices are not regulated and gas is sold in spot markets – primarily North America and the UK – fewer (if any) fiscal incentives are offered and the same fiscal regime applies to oil and gas production equally. This can create problems for investors if a significant divergence between oil and gas prices emerges in the spot markets. In a rising oil price environment, upstream costs tend to increase and most of these costs (e.g. drilling rig rates and fabrication rates for pipelines and production facilities) are the same for both gas and oil operations. But if gas prices do not rise as fast as oil, gas project economics will suffer in comparison.

There are a number of countries where fiscal terms have been agreed with investors for exploration and production of oil but contain no commercial terms for gas, such as many PSCs in West Africa. Investors who discover commercial quantities of gas may find that the government regards them as having no rights to the gas at all, and their involvement in the gas development will need to be gained, potentially in competition with other potential investors. In other situations, the oil investor may have the right to develop appropriate commercial terms with the government, but often the contract is silent as to the principles this should be based on.

Finally, an approach which can overcome many of the issues surrounding oil versus gas taxation is to develop fiscal terms which are linked to project profitability, such as profit sharing or tax rates linked to rate of return or 'R- factor' measures. These 'progressive' terms can apply to any individual project and will generate a high government take only from the most profitable projects. The arguments for and against the use of such fiscal regimes are made in more detail elsewhere in this volume. [1]

---

[1] Philip Daniel, Michael Keen and Charles McPherson: The Taxation of Petroleum and Minerals. international Monetary Fund. 2010. P 174: 176

6. Depreciation and Depletion in Oil Production

The answer to where and how a capital investment is spent is found through the following discussion. Economic analysis of the expenditures and revenues for oil operations requires recognition of two important facts:

1. Physical assets decrease in value with time, i.e., they *depreciate*.

2. Oil resources, like other natural resources, cannot be renewed over the years and they are continuously *depleted*.

Depreciation or amortization is described as the systematic allocation of the cost of an asset from the balance sheet to a depreciation expense on

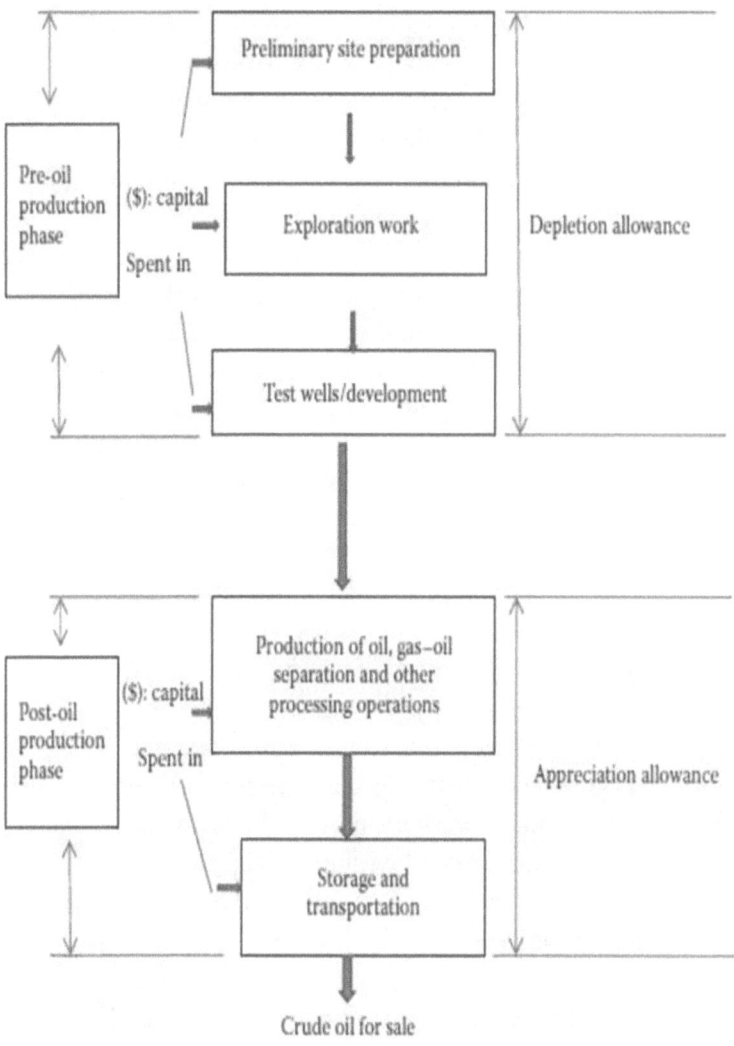

the income statement over the useful life of an asset. On the other hand, depletion allowance is a depreciation-like charge applied to account for the exhaustion of natural resources.

As shown in Figure 5.1, for oil production operations, we have two phases where capital investment has to be spent. The first phase, called the *pre–oil-production phase*, involves preliminary preparation, exploration, dry-well drilling, and development. The property is now ready for the second phase, where money is spent in providing necessary assets and equipment for the production stage and post–oil production. The question is: How can we recover the capital spent in the pre–oil-production phase and the *production/postproduction phase* as well?

For oil production operation, as seen in Section 1.9, capital investment is spent in two consecutive phases: the pre-production oil phase and the production/post-production oil phase. As far as the second phase, physical assets can be tangibly verified in a property; hence *depreciation accounting* can be applied to recover this capital investment. The *first* phase, on the other hand, exhibits the contrary: intangible costs were invested, because no physical assets can count for them. In this case, *depletion accounting* is introduced to recover the development costs that were spent for exploration and other preliminary operations prior to the actual production of oil and gas. In other words, depletion allowance is a depreciation-like charge applied to an account for the exhaustion of natural resources. [1]

6.1. Decommissioning

The economic lifetime of a project normally terminates once its net cash flow turns permanently negative, at which moment the field is decommissioned. Since towards the end of field life the capital spending and asset depreciation are generally negligible, economic decommissioning can be defined as the point at which gross income no longer covers operating costs (and royalties). It is of course still technically possible to continue producing the field, but at a financial loss.

Most companies have at least two ways in which to defer the decommissioning of a field or installation

(a) reduce the operating costs, or

(b) increase hydrocarbon throughput

In some cases, where production is subject to high taxation, tax concessions may be negotiated, but generally host Governments will expect all other means to have been investigated first.

---

[1]Hussein K. Abdel-Aal Mohamed A. Aggour Mohamed A. Fahim: Petroleum and Gas Field Processing. Second Edition. Taylor & Francis Group, LLC. 2016. P 78: 79

Maintenance and operating costs represent the major expenditure late in field life.

These costs will be closely related to the number of staff required to run a facility and the amount of hardware they operate to keep production going. The specifications for product quality and plant up-time can also have a significant impact on running costs.

As decommissioning approaches, enhanced recovery, for example chemical flooding processes are often considered as a means of recovering a proportion of the hydrocarbons that remain after primary production. The economic viability of such techniques is very sensitive to the oil price, and whilst some are used in onshore developments they can less often be justified offshore.

When production from the reservoir can no longer sustain running costs but the technical operating life of the facility has not expired, opportunities may be available to develop nearby reserves through the existing infrastructure. This has become increasingly common where the infrastructure already installed is being exploited to develop much smaller fields than would otherwise be possible. These fields are not necessarily owned by the company which operates the host facilities, in which case a service charge (tariff) will be negotiated for the use of third party facilities.

Ultimately, all economically recoverable reserves will be depleted and the field will be decommissioned. Much thought is now going into decommissioning planning to devise procedures which will minimize the environmental effects without incurring excessive cost. Steel platforms may be cut off to an agreed depth below sea level or toppled over in deep waters, whereas concrete structures may be refloated, towed away and sunk in the deep ocean. Pipelines may be flushed and left in place. In shallow tropical waters opportunities may exist to use decommissioned platforms and jackets as artificial reefs in a designated offshore area.

Management of decommissioning costs is an issue that most companies have to face at some time. On land sites, wells can often be plugged and processing facilities dismantled on a phased basis, thus avoiding high spending levels just as hydrocarbons run out. Offshore decommissioning costs can be very significant and less easily spread as platforms cannot be removed in a piecemeal fashion. The way in which provision is made for such costs depends partly on the size of the company involved and on the prevailing tax rules.

Usually a company will have a portfolio of assets which are at different stages of the described life cycle. Proper management of the asset base will allow optimization of financial, technical and human resources. [1]

---

[1] Frank Jahn, Mark Cook and Mark Graham: HYDROCARBON EXPLORATION AND PRODUCTION. 2ND EDITION. Elsevier B.V. 2008. P 6: 7

7. Renewable Energy Targets and Carbon Pricing May Conflict

Nearly, all CO2 schemes operate in parallel with other schemes, especially renewable energy targets. Although it is often assumed that the long-run effect of both policy instruments will be to encourage renewable energy, the policy instruments are targeting different metrics and distort the normal operation of the electricity market. For example, in Australia, PV operates outside of the normal dispatch queue without any direct control from system operators. Wind power operates within the normal market, but is operated on a must-take basis, regardless of prevailing market conditions.

In most cases, solar energy displaces lower-emission gas-fired generation rather than higher-emission coal-fired generation since coal-fired baseload resides at the bottom of the dispatch queue. Since solar PV only generates during the day, there will always be peak or intermediate load supply higher in the dispatch queue; hence, it mostly displaces generation that is already contributing to lowering the system emission intensity. In contrast, wind energy may also displace coal due to the prevalence of night-time wind (when the entire load is met with baseload), but thermal cycling may erode some of the emission gains of wind. In many scenarios, it is clear that policy prescriptions can seek to maximize renewable penetration or maximize abatement, but not both. [1]

7.1. Alternative Energy Sources

There are plenty of energy sources other than fossil fuels. Running out of energy in the long run is not the problem. The bind comes during the next 10 years: getting over our dependence on crude oil.

"Geothermal" energy is just what its name implies, heat recovered from within the Earth's crust. Just as with oil fields, there are a few high-grade geothermal areas, a larger number in the middle, and extensive low-grade heat sources that may not be economic in this century. Before 1960, three high-grade geothermal fields were generating electric power: Lardarello, Italy; the Geysers, north of San Francisco; and Wairakei, New Zealand (pronounced wy-RACK-ie). Each area was originally identified from hot springs at the surface, and ordinary oil-well-drilling technology was used to exploit the resource.

The water from these three areas was hot enough to boil, giving an impressive yield of

---

[1]Graham Palmer: Energy in Australia. Springer Cham Heidelberg New York Dordrecht London 2014. P 76

steam. Passing the steam through turbines generated electrical power; the steam was condensed back to water on the downstream side of the turbine to increase the energy yield. The Geysers geothermal field produces about half of the electricity used by the city of San Francisco. [1]

The beauty of a binary geothermal plant is zero emissions to the atmosphere and returning the water to the ground. You don't need an Environmental Protection Agency permit to pump arsenic, mercury, and antimony back into the ground if you just took the water out of an adjacent hole. The binary process opens a range of geothermal opportunities that would not otherwise be economic. [2]

Drilling for geothermal energy utilizes the same equipment and skills that were developed for the oil industry. It comes as no surprise that oil companies looked at geothermal resources as an extension of their existing activities. There are rumors that at least one major oil company is holding leases on U.S. geothermal areas as a way of extending its business into an era of energy shortage. [3]

---

[1] K E N N E T H S . D E F F E Y E S: Hubbert's Peak. Princeton University Press. 2001. P 176
[2] K E N N E T H S . D E F F E Y E S: Hubbert's Peak. Princeton University Press. 2001. P 178
[3] K E N N E T H S . D E F F E Y E S: Hubbert's Peak.

Similarly, the enriched-uranium, water-moderated nuclear reactor dominates the market for nuclear power plants. Actually, the standard commercial nuclear power reactors are derived from the U.S.

Navy nuclear submarine reactors. However, there are about a dozen fundamentally different designs for nuclear reactors. I once heard Eugene Wigner lecture on reactor designs. During World War II, Wigner designed the reactors at Hanford; later he won the Nobel Prize for bringing group theory into physics. Back when new power reactors were being built, the Canadians built and operated several reactors that used natural uranium and "heavy water" (deuterium) as the moderator that slowed down the neutrons. The Canadian deuterium reactors went by the overly clever name of CANDU. The CANDU reactors had an outstanding track record for reliability. I suspect that if we sat down today to reinvent the nuclear power industry, we might not choose the standard American design.

Reactors have two options for their used uranium. The spent fuel elements can be disposed of in their entirety as radioactive waste. Or the used uranium can be "reprocessed" to recover unburned uranium and to recover

Princeton University Press. 2001. P 179

plutonium. Plutonium is evil stuff. Besides being exceedingly toxic, plutonium can be used as the core of a nuclear bomb.

Ted Taylor, who was the leading American designer of nuclear weapons, left Los Alamos to campaign against nuclear proliferation because he felt that it was entirely too easy to build an effective nuclear bomb out of stolen plutonium. There is a continuing debate about whether you need a large staff of whizzbang scientists to build a nuclear weapon or whether you could build one in your garage. No question that Ted Taylor could build one in his garage.

Despite the scary aspect, some spent fuel from commercial power reactors has been reprocessed and the plutonium recycled for additional reactor fuel. A dilemma over reprocessing arose for the Australians around 1980. Huge uranium deposits had just been discovered in northern Australia; the Jabilinka deposit by itself contained more uranium that the United States had mined since 1940.6 The Australians preferred not to encourage worldwide growth of nuclear power plants. But as the specter of reprocessing and commercial plutonium shipments arose, the Australians switched their position. If Australian uranium is cheap enough, nobody will want to reprocess spent fuel. [1]

Solar and wind power participate in what I call the energy material paradox. If materials were cheap, I could build large energy collectors. If energy were cheap, I could produce large amounts of raw materials. If neither materials nor energy is cheap, I have a problem.

At the moment, solar and wind power are developing in specialized areas. Neither is an immediate, large-scale solution to the energy problem.

The power per square foot in the sunshine is essentially identical to the power per square foot in the wind. At first, I thought that this was just an accident, but solar energy may crank up the wind velocity until the average energy density in the wind equals the average solar energy density. Wind and sun don't appear together at the same place or the same time. As an example: wind often is stronger at a gap in the mountains. At the southern end of the Sierra Nevada, there is a huge array of windmills. They don't look like Dutch windmills, or like my

---

[1] K E N N E T H S . D E F F E Y E S: Hubbert's Peak. Princeton University Press. 2001. P 181: 182

grandmother's daisy wheel; they are slender, three-bladed propellers on tall stands.

The low energy density in solar and wind power requires large energy collectors. A normal-size nuclear or fossil-fuel power plant generates 1,000 megawatts. At typical efficiencies around 10 percent, a solar or wind collector has to occupy five square miles to deliver 1,000 megawatts. I can direct you to any of several Nevada basins where you can get the five square miles; your problem is the capital cost of paving five square miles with solar collectors. [1]

---

[1]K E N N E T H S . D E F F E Y E S: Hubbert's Peak. Princeton University Press. 2001. P 183

8. The Geopolitics of Oil

The impact of Israel has been only one of the elements affecting the political evolution of the Middle East in recent years. The control of the region's oil was perhaps the greater underlying element.

One of the first steps in this progression was the rise to power of Reza Shah Pahlavi in Iran in 1925, who aimed to modernize the country. He entertained certain sympathies for Germany in the Second World War and was forced to abdicate under British pressure in 1941 in favor of his son, Mohammad. The latter continued to rule in an autocratic manner, although pressures for a more liberal regime developed in the post-war years. [1]

The new political situation eventually threw up an ageing aristocrat by the name of Mohammad Mossadegh, whose party came to power in 1951. It felt that the time for change had come, and successfully passed a bill in Parliament for the nationalization of BP's exclusive Iranian concession. It was thought unjust that the company should deliver more to its shareholders than it paid to the country in whose land the oil lay.

---

[1]C.J. Campbell: Campbell's Atlas of Oil and Gas Depletion. Colin J. Campbell and Alexander Wöstmann 2013. P 382

This was not well received by Washington, which succeeded in influencing the Iranian army to depose him. Clearly, its control of a substantial percentage of world oil supply was a critical factor explaining why the nature of the government of this remote country should be of any particular interest. But the political pressure for change grew and erupted in the so-called Islamic Revolution of 1978–1979, which led to the fall of the Shah. This gave the Second Oil Shock as prices soared, prompted by panic buying as traders feared a resumption of shortage. The American Embassy was briefly occupied and hostages were taken in an effort to secure the return of the Shah for trial. Although negotiations subsequently resolved the issue, Iran came to be regarded as a hostile power by the United States. [1]

Meanwhile, Iraq under its President, Saddam Hussein, was in conflict with Iran over the demarcation of the frontier between the two countries. The problems lay in relation to both the oil-rich region of Khuzestan, a *Sunni* enclave, whose people had historical links with Iraq, and the critical Shattal- Arab waterway, which could give Iraq better access to the Persian Gulf, by-passing Kuwait. The frontiers had been arbitrarily drawn by Britain at the end

---

[1]C.J. Campbell: Campbell's Atlas of Oil and Gas Depletion. Colin J. Campbell and Alexander Wöstmann 2013. P 382

of the First World War as already described, so there may have been some historical justification for Iraq's position. The United States began to see Saddam Hussein as a useful ally in its opposition to Iran.

Hostilities between the two countries opened in 1980 and dragged on for six long years with appalling loss of life on both sides. Children were in some cases even used to clear mine fields. The United States supplied its new ally with arms, finance and intelligence. It is noteworthy that Saddam Hussein belonged to the *Sunni* sect of Islam, whereas most Iranians and the majority in Iraq itself belong to the *Shi'ah* sect. These religious divisions have had an important in fluence on Middle East politics. [1]

But the war coincided with a period of low oil prices, partly reflecting the development of the North Sea oil fields. As a result, the Organization of Petroleum Exporting Countries (OPEC) had difficulty in observing their agreed quotas to limit production to support price. In 1985, Kuwait, announced a 50% increase in its reported reserves on which quota was based, although nothing particular had changed in the oil fields. It also began to pump oil from its end

---

[1] C.J. Campbell: Campbell's Atlas of Oil and Gas Depletion. Colin J. Campbell and Alexander Wöstmann 2013. P 382

of the South Rumaila oil field that straddled the ill-defined boundary with Iraq, possibly taking some of Iraq's rightful share.

These actions gave Iraq legitimate reasons for complaint. It was, at the time, on friendly terms with the United States, whose Ambassador gave tacit support for a military solution, by issuing a statement to the effect that *border disputes between Arab countries were of no concern to the United States.* Saddam Hussein, evidently misreading the mandate for a limited action, mounted a full-scale invasion of Kuwait on 2nd August 1990.

This proved to be too much for Washington, which may have come to fear that Iraq might gain excessive power over oil supply. When diplomatic efforts failed, the United States mobilized an army under General Schwarzkopf to oust Iraq's troops from Kuwait. It successfully did so during the early months of 1991 in what was known as the First Gulf War, but not before the retreating Iraqi army had fi red the oil fields. Some 2 billion barrels of oil went up in smoke.

The army was however ordered to withdraw at the gates of Baghdad in recognition that further intervention would stir up a hornets' nest.

Saddam Hussein was no longer the good friend he had once been, and the United Nations was persuaded to impose sanctions limiting Iraq's oil exports. While causing much suffering to the Iraqi people, they had the effect of lifting world oil prices which was well received both in the oil fields of Texas and by the other OPEC. The sanctions were however relaxed from time to time *for humanitarian reasons* when prices rose uncomfortably high. [1]

In general, violent and militarized political incidents appear to have a negative impact on crude oil trade for exporters. Considering the difference between intrastate (i.e., domestic conflict that is contained within a country's borders) and interstate (i.e., cross-national conflict that involves at least two countries) political events, we find that domestic conflict poses a more consistent threat to crude oil trade. Additionally, we find that exports of crude oil from the GCC countries are especially vulnerable to cross-national conflict. The results are less clear for importers. Indeed, the results for Northeast Asia (NEA) are inconsistent compared to other countries in the sample. We find some evidence that the import of crude oil to NEA economies may be more sensitive to cross-national conflict than the rest of the

---

[1] C.J. Campbell: Campbell's Atlas of Oil and Gas Depletion. Colin J. Campbell and Alexander Wöstmann 2013. P 382: 383

sample, with a reduction in trade when NEA economies are involved in a cross-national dispute. Political disruption appears to play a bigger role in disruption of crude oil trade for exporters than for importers, though this may be an artefact of the differences in how we econometrically control for the baseline expectation for crude oil trade with importers versus exporters. [1]

Nonetheless, for exporters and importers, non-political variables explain the majority of variance for crude oil trade. Although we find that political events affect crude oil trade, particularly for exporters, they are not the dominant factor driving crude oil trade volumes. Economic and market forces appear to play a much larger role. In energy trade relations between the GCC and NEA, political instability should not be ignored, but the underlying economic fundamentals of the relationship are more crucial for ensuring energy security. [2]

As since the beginning of the 2000s, world oil prices started to rise steadily, therefore also increasing European gas prices, the

---

[1] Leo Lester: Energy Relations and Policy Making in Asia. 2016. P 204
[2] Leo Lester: Energy Relations and Policy Making in Asia. 2016. P 204

differential between European prices and those charged to the Commonwealth of Independent States (CIS) widened sharply. Gazprom called for CIS prices to be raised to the level of European netback, while all countries struggled to increase domestic gas pricing. Th e Russian government influence was responsible for the netback principle to be applied unevenly. Countries that agreed to share ownership of their pipeline system with Russia (e.g. Belarus and Armenia) were able to negotiate much longer timetables for import price increases. On the other hand, Gazprom was allowed to raise prices more rapidly in countries whose governments showed a hostile attitude toward Moscow (e.g. Georgia and Ukraine).

But it was not until January 2006, one year after the Orange Revolution had taken place in Ukraine, which resulted in a strongly pro-Western and anti-Russian Government, that the first major Ukraine-Russia gas crises erupted in January 2006. Following disagreement on prices, Russia cut off supplies to Ukraine for three days, Ukraine diverted volumes destined to Europe, and as a consequence, supply to some Central European countries fell briefly, but supplies were never cut off completely on that occasion. Due to the pro-European government in Kiev, the EU was fully supporting Ukraine and strongly blaming Russia for the crisis. [1]

The second major gas crises between Russia, Ukraine and Europe of January 2009 became a very high-profile event. As a result of this crisis, the transit of Russian gas through Ukraine was completely cut for two weeks, which resulted in humanitarian crises in several Central and Eastern European countries that were strongly dependent on Russian gas supplies across Ukraine. Th is dispute has resulted in long-term economic consequences and affected the reputation of Russia as a reliable supplier and of Ukraine as a reliable transit country. The policy responses to these gas crises were different in Europe, Ukraine and Russia.

Russia's response to the crises was first to push for ownership of the Ukrainian transit system by a consortium involving Ukrainian, Russian and European gas companies. As it became increasingly clear that this option was not acceptable to Ukraine, Russia launched a strategy of diversification of its gas transit routes to Europe, away from Ukraine.

The EU's response, particularly to the major crises of 2006 and 2009, was to strengthen the internal market, to foster gas flows and gas sources diversification (including building LNG

[1] Simone Tagliapietra: Energy Relations in the Euro-Mediterranean. 2017. P 67: 68

receiving terminals in Central and South-East Europe, pursuing climate change policies (energy efficiency, renewables, clean coal with carbon capture and storage technologies, nuclear) and, particularly developing an SGC to evacuate new Caspian and Middle Eastern gas supplies to Europe via Turkey. The genesis and the evolution of this Corridor will be widely discussed in the next section. [1]

So, what is it that the Americans, the Russians and the Chinese really want from the Middle East in the 21st century? Once this question is answered, everything becomes very simple. The US has increased its oil imports from Canada, Mexico, Venezuela, even from Russia, while at the same time it has increased its own oil and natural gas production too, and as a result it has drastically reduced its oil imports from the Middle East. Therefore, the US is not dependent on the Middle East for oil in the same way it has been in the past, which was to a large extent what determined the US policies in the Middle East during the 20th century. [2]

---

[1] Simone Tagliapietra: Energy Relations in the Euro-Mediterranean. 2017. P 68: 69
[2] Iakovos Alhadeff: USA Russia & China in the Middle East. Free ebook.net 2014. P 4

8.1. The Financial Impact of Terrorist Attacks on the Value of the Oil and Gas Industry

According to START's Global Terrorism Database, the number of terrorist attacks on companies in the utility sector is increasing. Karolyi and Martell (2010) argue that information about terrorist attacks can induce investors to demand either a higher risk premium or flee the market searching for more stable financial assets. It is relevant for both the investors as well as for the companies to know about the effect of terrorist attacks on company returns. Previous studies on the effect of terrorism on financial markets focuses mainly on major terrorist events or the effect of general terrorist events on stock prices of industries or even the stock market as a whole. However, these studies do not account for potential differences in sensitivity and vulnerability of different industries. Furthermore, they tend to be biased as they mainly investigate terrorist attacks on 'western' corporations. Our research focuses on terrorist attacks on international oil and gas companies. We do conduct an event study to detect the impact of these attacks on the stock market return of the corporations. We look into different subsamples of the data to investigate interesting cross-sectional characteristics, such as firms that are hit incidentally versus those that are hit more frequently. [1]

We investigate the effects of terrorism on the stock market returns of corporations in the oil and gas industry, i.e. the financial market perspective regarding terrorism. This is important from the perspective of strategic risk management. We analyze 105 terrorist attacks aimed at oil and gas companies in the period 2001–2012. We hypothesize that companies that are the target of a terrorist attack will experience an abnormal return at the event date or in the two days after the attack. Previous literature suggests either zero or negative returns. For the energy companies studied, we were not able to detect a significant response of the stock market returns to terrorist attacks. This result is in line with Suleman (2012) and partly with that of Kollias et al. (2013), but contrasts with less focused and older studies. We do find that companies that are attacked more often react significantly different from companies that are attacked less often. Furthermore, it appears as if investors in energy firms seem to be almost getting used to terrorism, because they react significantly less negative in 2011–2012 compared to 2001–2007. This in fact suggests that financial market participants come to view terrorism regarding energy firms as a 'fact of life' and seem to assume that firms already efficiently manage the threat of terrorism in the

---

[1] Andre´ Dorsman • O¨ zg€ur Arslan-Ayaydin • Mehmet Baha Karan: Energy and Finance. Springer International Publishing Switzerland 2016. P 71

energy industry (Karolyi and Martell 2010). Overall, we conclude that financial markets seem to be efficient in absorbing the impact of terrorist attacks. [1]

From a policy perspective, our findings do not infer that one should not worry about attacks on energy companies. Cities, regions or countries—and, of course, especially the people living there—may be vulnerable to terrorist attacks (Lilliestam 2014). However, the protection of energy firms as such need not be the first priority in energy security. In contrast, it seems that protecting vulnerable infrastructure would be short-term priority, whereas switching to resilient energy systems is a long-term strategy. Here, energy companies have an important role to play as they are key actors in the transition to a more resilient energy system. [2]

8.2. The Militarization of Energy (In)Security

The relationship between energy availability, national security, and the use of force first took shape during World War I, when

---

[1]Andre' Dorsman • O" zgєur Arslan-Ayaydin • Mehmet Baha Karan: Energy and Finance. Springer International Publishing Switzerland 2016. P 78

[2]Andre' Dorsman • O" zgєur Arslan-Ayaydin • Mehmet Baha Karan: Energy and Finance. Springer International Publishing Switzerland 2016. P 78

oil-powered weapons— notably tanks, planes, and submarines—made their initial appearance on the battlefield. With few sources of petroleum then in production, mostly concentrated in the USA, Romania, Iran (then Persia), and Baku in Czarist Russia, the belligerents sought to control these areas or deny them to their opponents.

Believing that possession of abundant supplies of oil would be essential for success in any future contests of this magnitude, the surviving great powers engaged in a competitive struggle to extend their control over the major oil producing areas. Th e major European states, possessing few domestic reserves of their own, largely focused their efforts on acquiring concessions in the oil-bearing regions of the Middle East. This was the era of the San Remo Agreement of 1920, under which Britain obtained control over Iraq and France of Syria under mandates from the League of Nations. Meanwhile, Japan—a rising industrial power with a similar paucity of oil—harbored imperial ambitions over the Dutch East Indies, then the major oil producer in Asia.

As World War II approached, the need to secure overseas sources of oil to sustain both industrial and military operations played a significant role in the strategic planning of Germany and Japan, both of which feared the consequences of inadequate domestic supplies. In 1941, when full-scale combat broke out, both countries undertook military strikes with this purpose in mind: Germany invaded the Soviet Union, with Baku as one of its primary objectives; Japan invaded the Dutch East Indies. And, because Tokyo feared that its invasion of the Dutch East Indies would provoke a US military response—particularly, a naval drive to starve Japan of oil—it simultaneously attacked the US naval base at Pearl Harbor in Hawaii, thus ensuring American entry into the war.

Until this point, the USA had not participated in the strategic (as distinct from the commercial) pursuit of overseas oil, as it possessed sufficient domestic reserves to satisfy its wartime military requirements and those of its principal allies. As World War II progressed, however, President Franklin D. Roosevelt and his senior advisers worried that the heavy wartime exploitation of domestic oil was rapidly depleting US reserves, eroding America's capacity to sustain another full-scale war on the magnitude of World War II. Accordingly, Roosevelt ordered the State and Commerce Departments to seek a reliable foreign source of oil to supplement American reserves in the event of a future conflict. After considering the various possibilities, government experts concluded in 1943 that Saudi Arabia represented the best candidate to serve in this capacity. With this in mind, Roosevelt met with King Abdul Aziz ibn Saud on February 14, 1945, and forged an agreement with him under which the USA would obtain privileged access to Saudi oil in return for an American pledge to protect the monarchy against its assorted enemies.

In the years that followed, the USA became ever more deeply involved in Persian Gulf affairs. Following London's 1968 decision to withdraw all British forces from the region by 1972, President Richard Nixon chose Iran—then controlled by Shah Mohammed Reza Pahlavi—to serve as a substitute 'gendarme' in the Gulf and, in accordance with this plan, agreed to provide the Iranians with a vast array of modern American weapons. Later, after the Soviets invaded Afghanistan and the Shah was overthrown, President Jimmy Carter concluded that the USA could no longer rely on surrogates but would have to assume direct responsibility for ensuring the safety of Persian Gulf oil supplies.

Th is stance was first articulated in his State of the Union address of January 23, 1980 and has been known since as the Carter Doctrine. 'Let our position be absolutely clear,' he declared. 'An attempt by any outside force to gain control of the Persian Gulf region will be regarded as an assault on the vital interests of the

United States of America, and such an assault will be repelled by any means necessary, including military force'.

Because the USA did not at that time possess any forces specifically earmarked for operations in the Gulf area, Carter also created a new military organization—the Rapid Deployment Joint Task Force (RDJTF)—to provide this function.

Carter's successor, President Ronald Reagan, elevated the RDJTF into a region-wide military organization, the US Central Command, and tasked it with protection of the oil flow from the Gulf area. Reagan was also the first American president to fully implement the Carter Doctrine: when Iranian forces attacked Kuwaiti tankers during the Iran–Iraq War of 1980–88, he determined that such action constituted a severe threat to the free flow of oil and authorized the 'reflagging' of those tankers with the American ensign, thereby allowing their protection by the US Navy (Palmer 1992). Th e protection of Persian Gulf oil was also cited by Reagan's successor, President George H.W. Bush, as the justification for US eff orts to protect Saudi Arabia following the Iraqi invasion of Kuwait on August 2, 1990.

Although the Persian Gulf area has long been the principal focus of US eff orts to ensure the safety of foreign energy supplies, American leaders— fearing overdependence on one often-imperiled source of supply—have also sought to increase reliance on other foreign producing areas. Th is drive, known as 'diversification,' has, in particular, focused on the procurement of additional oil from the Caspian Sea basin and West Africa, both considered attractive new producing zones. But while attractive as alternatives, these areas also harbor threats to the safe flow of oil—and so growing reliance on their hydrocarbon output has led to increased US military involvement in both areas.

Th e Caspian Sea basin first attracted widespread interest in the early 1990s, following the breakup of the Soviet Union. Until then, oil production in this region was under the control of central planners in Moscow and there was little opportunity for local firms or foreign companies to become involved; after the Soviet breakup, however, the energy-rich states of the Caspian region—Azerbaijan, Kazakhstan, Turkmenistan, and Uzbekistan—opened their countries to foreign investment, usually in conjunction with state-owned companies. This resulted, before long, in the establishment of several major international consortia for the extraction and export of the region's copious energy resources.

Viewing these undertakings as a substantial contribution to the diversification of Western energy imports, US leaders vowed to do whatever they could to facilitate their success. By promoting Caspian exports, President Bill Clinton told his Azerbaijani counterpart, Heydar Aliyev, 'we not only help Azerbaijan to prosper, but also help diversify our energy supply and strengthen our nation's security. In consonance with this outlook, Clinton worked closely with Aliyev and other Caspian officials to construct the Baku–Tbilisi–Ceyhan (BTC) pipeline from Azerbaijan across the Caucasus to Turkey (thereby bypassing both Russia and Iran as transit states) and to bolster their self-defense capabilities in the face of widespread regional instability. Clinton's successor, President George W. Bush, also placed a high priority on securing access to Caspian oil and gas, backing local leaders in their efforts to resist domination by Moscow and providing stepped up military assistance.

A similar trajectory of increased US involvement can be seen in the oil producing areas of West Africa. Keen to reduce US reliance on the Persian Gulf area and to increase drilling opportunities for American oil firms, the

George W. Bush administration placed particular emphasis on increased US energy investment there. But, as in the Caspian area and the Gulf, such eff orts were imperiled by widespread violence and instability. Accordingly, Washington expanded its military aid and training programs for friendly local governments.

To help sustain and manage these endeavors, President Bush authorized the establishment of yet another new military organization, the US Africa Command (Africom), in 2007—much as President Carter followed the enunciation of his famous doctrine of January 1980 with the creation of (what became) the US Central Command.

The drive to diversify US sources of imported oil was largely intended to diminish the nation's dependence on Persian Gulf oil, and thereby minimize the risks and complications of American involvement in that chronically unstable area. By turning to the Caspian region and Africa, however, the USA did not escape the security dimensions of reliance on imported energy.

In fact, these areas harbored many of the same sorts of internal fissures as those encountered in the Gulf, and so again

Washington found it necessary to respond with military measures of one type or another. Because the BTC pipeline crosses through Georgia, passing near such war-torn areas as Chechnya and South Ossetia, the Clinton and Bush administrations provided substantial military aid to Georgia's military forces, at some points stationing large military training contingents there (OGJ 2003). Similarly, President Bush found it necessary to increase US arms and training aid to Africa, particularly to Nigeria and other states bordering the oil-rich Gulf of Guinea. [1]

---

[1] Thijs Van de Graaf • Benjamin K. Sovacool Arunabha Ghosh • Florian Kern • Michael T. Klare: The Palgrave Handbook of the International Political Economy of Energy. 2016. P 422: 425

References

1. Andre´ Dorsman • O¨ zg€ur Arslan-Ayaydin • Mehmet Baha Karan: Energy and Finance. Springer International Publishing Switzerland 2016.
2. Andre´ Dorsman • Timur Go¨k • Mehmet Baha Karan: Perspectives on Energy Risk. Springer-Verlag Berlin Heidelberg 2014.
3. C.J. Campbell: Campbell's Atlas of Oil and Gas Depletion. Colin J. Campbell and Alexander Wöstmann 2013.
4. Charles A.S. Hall: Energy Return on Investment. 2017.
5. Congrui Jin • Gianluca Cusatis: New Frontiers in Oil and Gas Exploration. Springer International Publishing Switzerland 2016.
6. Cyrus Bina: A Prelude to the Foundation of Political Economy. PALGRAVE MACMILLAN. 2013.
7. Dagmar Sibyl Steuwer: Energy Efficiency Governance. Springer Fachmedien Wiesbaden 2013.
8. enerdata: American (shale) gas, the new benchmark for energy prices?.2016.
9. Frank Jahn, Mark Cook and Mark Graham: HYDROCARBON EXPLORATION AND PRODUCTION. 2ND EDITION. Elsevier B.V. 2008.
10. Graham Palmer: Energy in Australia. Springer Cham Heidelberg New York Dordrecht London 2014.

11. Hussein K. Abdel-Aal Mohamed A. Aggour Mohamed A. Fahim: Petroleum and Gas Field Processing. Second Edition. Taylor & Francis Group, LLC. 2016.
12. Iakovos Alhadeff: USA Russia & China in the Middle East. Free ebook.net 2014.
13. Irwin A. Wiehe: Process Chemistry of Petroleum Macromolecules. Taylor & Francis Group, LLC. 2008.
14. J. Edward Gates • David L. Trauger • Brian Czech: Peak Oil, Economic Growth, and Wildlife Conservation. Springer Science+Business Media New York 2014.
15. KENNETH S. DEFFEYES: Hubbert's Peak. Princeton University Press. 2001.
16. Leo Lester: Energy Relations and Policy Making in Asia. 2016.
17. Ming Yang • Xin Yu: Energy Efficiency Benefits for Environment and Society. Springer-Verlag London 2015.
18. Naoyuki Yoshino • Farhad Taghizadeh-Hesary: Monetary Policy and the Oil Market. Asian Development Bank Institute 2016.
19. Nazim Muradov: Liberating Energy from Carbon: Introduction to Decarbonization. Springer Science+Business Media New York 2014.
20. Nuno Luis Madureira: Key Concepts in Energy. Springer International Publishing Switzerland 2014.

21. Philip Daniel, Michael Keen and Charles McPherson: The Taxation of Petroleum and Minerals. international Monetary Fund. 2010.
22. Roger Boyd: Energy and the Financial System Springer Cham Heidelberg New York Dordrecht London 2013.
23. Rossella Bardazzi • Maria Grazia Pazienza Alberto Tonini: European Energy and Climate Security. Springer International Publishing Switzerland 2016.
24. Salvatore Carollo: Understanding Oil Prices A John Wiley & Sons, Ltd., Publication. 2012.
25. Simone Tagliapietra: Energy Relations in the Euro-Mediterranean. 2017.
26. Thijs Van de Graaf • Benjamin K. Sovacool Arunabha Ghosh • Florian Kern • Michael T. Klare: The Palgrave Handbook of the International Political Economy of Energy. 2016.
27. Yi-Ming Wei • Hua Liao: Energy Economics: Energy Efficiency in China. Springer International Publishing Switzerland 2016.
28. Yulia Veld-Merkoulova • Svetlana Viteva: Carbon Finance. Springer International Publishing Switzerland 2016.

Biography of the author

Roshdy Ebrahim Abdin, Egyptian.

Ph.D (economics)

Economics lecturer.

Member at the Egyptian assembly for political economy.

Member at the Egyptian assembly for international law.

Professional diploma in arbitration.

diploma in importing and exporting.

Lawyer since 2008.

For more information please subscribe to my blog:

http://roshdyebrahim.blogspot.com.eg/

the author's books
1. Economic study of Oil and Gas Well Drilling
2. Economic study of Oil and Gas Exploration
3. Economics of oil and gas production
4. Economics of Petroleum, principles
5. Economics of petroleum reservoirs
6. Economics of petroleum market

www.ingramcontent.com/pod-product-compliance
Lightning Source LLC
Chambersburg PA
CBHW031621210526
45464CB00004B/1692